McGraw-Hill's

CAREERS FOR

HOMEBODIES

& Other Independent Souls

Careers for You Series

McGraw-Hill's

CAREERS FOR

HOMEBODIES

& Other Independent Souls

JAN GOLDBERG

SECOND EDITION

McGraw Hill

New York Chicago San Francisco Lisbon London Madrid Mexico City
Milan New Delhi San Juan Seoul Singapore Sydney Toronto

The *McGraw·Hill* Companies

Library of Congress Cataloging-in-Publication Data

Goldberg, Jan.
    Careers for homebodies & other independent souls / by Jan Goldberg —
2nd ed.
        p.   cm. — (McGraw-Hill careers for you series)
      ISBN 0-07-147616-4 (alk. paper)
      1. Home-based businesses—Vocational guidance.   2. Small business—
Vocational guidance. I. Title.   II. Title: Careers for homebodies and other
independent souls.

HD2341.G56 2007
331.702—dc2   2006028908

1 2 3 4 5 6 7 8 9 10 11 12 13 14 15   DOC/DOC   0 9 8 7

ISBN-13: 978-0-07-147616-4
ISBN-10:   0-07-147616-4

McGraw-Hill books are available at special quantity discounts to use as premiums and
sales promotions, or for use in corporate training programs. For more information,
please write to the Director of Special Sales, Professional Publishing, McGraw-Hill,
Two Penn Plaza, New York, NY 10121-2298. Or contact your local bookstore.

This book is printed on acid-free paper.

*This book is dedicated to the memory
of my very special and beloved parents,
Sam and Sylvia Lefkovitz.*

Contents

Acknowledgments

The author gratefully acknowledges the following individuals for their contributions:

- The numerous professionals who graciously agreed to be profiled in this book
- My dear husband, Larry, for his inspiration and vision
- My children—Sherri, Deborah, and Bruce—for their encouragement and love
- Family and close friends—Adrienne, Marty, Mindi, Cary, Michele, Paul, Michele, Alison, Steve, Marci, Steve, Brian, Steven, Jesse, Collin, Andrew, Bertha, Aunt Helen—for their faith and support
- Diana Catlin for her insights and input
- Blythe Camenson and Lillie Yvette Salinas for their continuing support

The editors would like to thank Josephine Scanlon for her work on this revision.

CHAPTER ONE

Are You an Independent Soul?

When work is pleasure, life is a joy!
When work is a duty, life is slavery.
—Maxim Gorky

N ow is a wonderful time to be thinking about working from home! With the tremendous opportunities made possible by the Web, it's easier now than ever before to work from home, whether in the capacity of freelancer, consultant, business owner, franchise operator, or telecommuter.

Apparently many people have discovered this. There are more than forty million home-working households in the United States, including about twenty-four million people who are running home-based businesses. People with home offices spend more than $30 billion annually on hardware and software and even more on telephone services. Home offices account for about 70 percent of all U.S. households on the Internet.

Studies indicate that, in general, the work-at-home market is affluent and well educated. Home-business owners are likely to have college and postgraduate degrees. Once you have read this book and the personal accounts of the homebodies profiled in the following chapters, you'll see that a combination of education, work experience, and a bit of a nest egg will serve you well in starting a home-based business.

Working at Home

Today there are more opportunities open to those of us who wish to have home-based careers than ever before. Such careers could take any one of several forms:

- Starting and running your own business
- Purchasing and operating a franchise
- Consulting or freelancing—both forms of self-employment
- Telecommuting, which means you work from home but are employed by someone else

All of these options share some common elements, but there are also ways in which they differ. In the following chapters we'll explore a number of these possibilities. And for those of you who are considering establishing your own businesses, we'll talk about how to choose a business and how to write a business plan.

Working at home requires a particular set of skills and a specific mind-set. Do you think your abilities and temperament are well suited to working at home? Take the following quiz, and you might gain some interesting insights into the question: do you have the right personality to work at home?

1. Are you self-motivated?
2. Can you avoid distractions?
3. Are you organized?
4. Are you self-disciplined?
5. Are you detail minded?
6. Are you serious about succeeding at this business endeavor?
7. Are you focused?
8. Can you juggle many aspects of projects and/or many projects at one time?
9. Are you good at marketing and selling—particularly selling yourself?

10. Are you able to switch hats to meet the necessity of the job at hand—for example, from marketing professional to salesperson to successful worker?
11. Are you an independent person?
12. Are you an able communicator?
13. Are you good at meeting deadlines?
14. Are you capable of prioritizing work?
15. Are you good at managing your time?
16. Are you flexible?
17. Are you able to work alone without feeling isolated?
18. Are you proficient at using the Web?
19. Are you familiar with fax machines and other kinds of office equipment?
20. Do you have an area in your home that would lend itself to becoming a home office—one that is separate and distinct from the rest of the house?

If you can honestly answer yes to most of these questions, you might have what it takes to be a successful homebody. Read on!

CHAPTER TWO

Getting Ready to Launch Your Business

*The work of the individual still remains the spark
that moves mankind ahead even more than teamwork.*

—Igor Sikorsky

Are you an avid sculptor who would love to share your master-pieces with the world? Are you an inspired cook who thinks your pasta would stand up to the highest scrutiny of world-renowned chefs? Are you (like me) a writer who feels compelled to play with words and ideas and communicate them to others? Are you a sports fanatic who wants to share that love through a business on the Web?

All of these individuals—and a seemingly endless stream of others—could start successful home-based businesses. (Note: even though all of your time may not be spent in your home office, as long as your office serves as "command central" for your enterprise, yours may still be considered a home-based business.)

Do you think you have what it takes to own and operate your own home-based business? Not everyone would fare well in this position, but if you had positive responses to the Chapter 1 quiz, you're probably on the right track. Many experts have found that a large number of successful small-business owners often have particular characteristics in common, including many of the following:

- Small-business owners are confident and believe strongly in their abilities and their ideas for success.
- They are goal setters who are able to pinpoint what they want and how they must go about achieving their goals.
- Small-business owners are usually willing to take calculated risks.
- They are either knowledgeable about their businesses from past experiences or determined to learn everything they can about their new fields.
- They know just where to go to seek help if they need business advice.
- Business owners are organized and capable of juggling a number of projects at the same time.
- They possess good business sense.
- Many come from families of home-based business owners, whether following in the same field or taking the skills learned in the family business and applying them to a new endeavor.
- They are usually good money managers.
- Home-business owners are patient and know how to persevere.
- They possess strong social skills and are able to deal comfortably with a wide variety of people.
- Business owners are flexible and have no problem with going back to the drawing board if it appears that something is not working.
- They have boundless energy and are driven to succeed.
- Business owners are intuitive and are good at making decisions.
- In many ways, business owners are courageous.

What's the Best Business for You?

How do you decide what type of business to pursue? One way is to examine your interests, hobbies, and strengths and try to build on one or more of those. Perhaps you can transfer skills you've developed from previous experiences to your business. Here are some possible avenues to explore:

- Think about all of the jobs—including volunteer positions and part-time jobs—that you've held over the years and what skills you've learned in them.
- Consider all of the clubs that you've joined and try to remember all of the activities that you've participated in.
- Have you had any valuable education or training that would qualify you for a particular business?
- Have you gained experience with school groups, church committees, fund-raising, organization support, family support groups, or group leadership?

Write down all of the applicable information and examine it to see if there are any patterns. Note all the things you liked about past positions, and pay particular attention to those areas that made the most of your skills. Seeing it all in writing might provide insight about a direction for you to explore.

Does the business you're considering require additional formal schooling or training? If it does, find out about any degrees, certifications, or special training that you'll need; consider how long it will take to complete the training and how much it will cost. In some situations, additional credentials will give you added stature in your business.

In selecting a business, feel free to think up something new and different or look for a new twist on a standard idea. Remember, don't be afraid to brainstorm for business ideas and to search for your particular niche.

Advantages of Working at Home

The last decade saw growth in the number of home-based workers that exceeded even the most aggressive projections. We are in an era of entrepreneurship, characterized by dramatic increases in the number of home offices. There has never been a better time to start a home-based business.

Working from home is attractive to people for many reasons. Running a home-based business lets mothers have more time with their children. Many people who have been the victims of downsizing and find it difficult to land another interesting position decide to turn their situation into something positive by striking out on their own. Still others work for employers who allow them to telecommute. And many are fulfilling a lifelong dream, whether it is to offer a particular service that they believe in or simply to be their own boss.

Although running a home office involves financial commitment, you are usually able to write off many, if not most, of your business expenses. In cases where the entire amount is not deductible, you can generally write off a percentage. Expenses in this category include supplies, professional help, insurance, mileage, services such as carpet cleaning and electrical work, property taxes, telephone, and utilities.

What are some of the other advantages of working from home?

- You have personal control over all decisions (if you enter into a partnership, then this control is shared with your partner).
- You don't have to pay office rent.
- Overhead costs are usually minimal.
- There is no commute to work, saving you time, money, and hassle.
- You can be independent.
- You can establish a home business in almost any field.

- In many fields, you can work from virtually anywhere in the country with the support of the Internet, fax lines, and express shipping.
- You can be closer to your family.
- You can manage your own time to maximize your productivity and balance your work and family life as you see fit.
- You can dress any way you wish—no dress codes here!
- You can work the hours and days you choose (within the limitations of your particular situation).
- Your schedule is your own—you can work in the middle of the night or schedule time off as needed.
- You can oversee or conduct all client contacts.
- You can set your own agenda.
- You earn all of the profits (or share them, in the case of a partnership).
- Home-based businesses are fully accepted and respected as legitimate businesses, now more than ever before.
- There is a wealth of information and support available from various groups and agencies.

Disadvantages of Working from Home

Although working from home might sound like a dream come true, it does have some disadvantages. What follows are a few of the downsides:

- There is no escape from the work—whatever you have to do is right there, and no one else will pick up the slack if you don't get it done.
- It's easy to be sidetracked by other concerns, such as doing household chores or running errands.
- Children, neighbors, family, and friends may well be steady distractions.
- There is no support team in place to help you out.

- You may have little or no direct contact with colleagues.
- You may feel very isolated.
- There is no paid vacation time, paid holidays, or paid sick leave.
- You are responsible for your own health insurance coverage and retirement plans.
- Frustration and stress are possible because you are solely responsible for the business.
- Income may be sporadic.

As mentioned earlier, working at home requires a very specific mind-set. Starting and operating a business is a major undertaking that should not be underestimated. There are issues of motivation and self-discipline, efficient time management, and balance between personal, family, and work obligations. Handling everything involved can be difficult; be sure that you have an outlet for stress. Despite these challenges, for millions of people, working at home is a dream come true.

First Things First

Before you even think of moving forward with your home-based business idea, you need to ask yourself a number of very pertinent questions to make sure that you are making a wise move. The better your planning, the more likely your success.

What Product or Service Will You Offer?

You have to do your homework to determine what it is you wish to offer, who your target audience is (those who are most likely to buy), and what your sales goals are.

Where Will You Work?

Sometimes this question is easily answered based on the type of business you plan to start. For example, if you are planning to set up a child-care center, then, of course, the children will be coming to you. However, if you're planning to set up a bookkeeping service, you'll probably be traveling to see your clients at their business sites. You may be able to arrange to have them come to you, but then you must understand that you'll need to have adequate parking for your clients and ideally a separate entrance to your work premises, as well as an appropriate place in your home to conduct meetings.

Whether you travel to your clients or they come to you, you'll need to set up a home office that is stocked with all of the equipment you'll need to run an efficient operation.

Your Work Space. Your home office needn't be luxurious or spacious or even very attractive, but it's certainly nice if it is. In truth, however, when you are starting out, your work space can be a corner, a closet, an attic area, or a basement nook. Just remember that you'll be spending a lot of time there, and the more attractive and comfortable it is, the more you'll be inclined to want to spend time there—a definite plus for the success of your enterprise. A comfortable space will go a long way toward making you feel more positive and work more efficiently to get your business off the ground.

Though it doesn't need to be expensive, it is vitally important that your working space look professional. This accomplishes a dual purpose. It puts you in a serious frame of mind, encouraging success in your efforts, and it creates a boundary between you and whatever is going on in the rest of the house that may distract you. When you are in your office, you are primed for work—no matter what is going on elsewhere. It shows anyone who comes to your office that you are a serious professional operating a real business.

Outfitting Your Office. You need to decide what equipment is necessary for you to begin this new career, and then you must figure out if you want to purchase new or used items. Some people start out with a bare-bones budget, and for them, picking up secondhand merchandise is probably a good idea.

One thing that you should arrange first is the installation of a separate business phone line. Once you've accomplished that, you need to decide whether you're going to purchase an answering machine, contract with an answering service, or arrange for voice mail. You might even look into using a combination of these possibilities. Just be sure to set up a system that enables you to be available to your clients. This is particularly imperative for a new business owner. Multifunction units that serve as telephone, answering machine, printer, scanner, and copy machine are a great way to save money.

You most likely already have a cell phone, which is a necessity if your business will take you out of the office on a regular basis. It's just too important that you not miss any calls. If people can't reach you, you may miss out on important contacts. If customers can't reach you, you definitely stand to lose their business.

Keep in mind that once established, you'll need to purchase office supplies on an ongoing basis. The large chain office-supply stores carry everything you will need for your home office. To save time, you can shop online at sites such as www.staples.com or www.officedepot.com. In-store services include copy centers where you can make your own copies at reasonable rates. Printing centers such as Kinko's can print documents from most disks and can even provide videoconferencing service for meetings.

If you are a telecommuter, your employer should pay for your office supplies. Some home-based workers send e-mail or fax requests for expensive supplies such as toner and cartridges to their employer, who will arrange for items to be shipped to the employee. Most telecommuters purchase smaller items themselves and submit receipts for reimbursement. Some recommend keeping one credit card strictly for office-related expenses; this makes it easier for both you and the supervisor who monitors your expenditures.

Is It Legal to Work from Home?

Though it is not a common occurrence, some towns or cities have certain restrictions pertaining to home businesses. Before you do anything else, make sure that you don't have to apply for any special licenses or permits.

Some states have regulations concerning how a particular business may operate, such as a day care center. In this case, the number of children you can handle may be limited, the equipment in your home may need to fit certain criteria, and the hours you can offer your services might be regulated. You may need to apply for a special license and meet other specifications via home inspection. Check with your state department of health or social services or call your local state senator or representative to find out how you need to proceed. Home-improvement contractors are often required to be licensed; the same is often the case for electricians and plumbers. Most state and local governments maintain websites where this information is readily available.

The appendixes offer a wide variety of resources to explore for more information, including associations, books, magazines, and websites.

Believe It or Not!

Here are some interesting stories surrounding the beginnings of some companies you have, no doubt, heard of. Believe it or not, they all started as home-based companies!

Rich DeVos and Jay Van Andel, Amway

Rich DeVos and Jay Van Andel, Amway's founders, hold a longtime friendship going all the way back to the time when Rich approached Jay with the idea of paying him twenty-five cents a week for a ride to school. After high school they entered the military but planned to start a business together after completing their separate tours of duty. This business became Amway.

In the 1960s, Amway quickly outgrew its original facilities in the basements of their homes. In a short time, the company began moving toward record figures. The 1980s will be remembered for including the first billion-dollar year at estimated retail. Building expansion at Amway World Headquarters continued at breakneck speed as the company scrambled to keep pace with demand. Today, Amway operates in more than eighty countries and territories and is part of the Alticor group of companies.

Most people who sell for Amway don't become billionaires, but founders Richard DeVos and Jay Van Andel did!

Ben Cohn and Jerry Greenfield, Ben and Jerry's Ice Cream

Ben Cohn and Jerry Greenfield, founders of Ben and Jerry's Ice Cream, were childhood friends. After enrolling in a Penn State ice cream–making correspondence course and with a $12,000 investment ($4,000 of which was borrowed), they began their fledgling company in 1978.

The partners converted a gas station into their first ice cream store and eventually made their way to the highest ranks in the ice cream industry. Becoming popular for their innovative flavors, made from fresh Vermont milk and cream, they were the ones to bring "Lemongrad" to Moscow and "Economic Chunk" to Wall Street.

The company grew to be considered one of the premier ice cream companies and in 1999 was purchased by Unilever. It now has markets in the United Kingdom, France, Benelux, Canada, Lebanon, and Japan.

William and Andrew Smith, Smith Brothers

Smith Brothers Cough Drop packaging portrays one of the world's most famous trademarks. The two bearded gentlemen who distinguish it, affectionately known to generations as Trade and Mark, are legendary. Not well known, however, is the fact that the Smith Brothers actually existed. Their names were William (Trade) and Andrew (Mark), and they helped found Smith Brothers in Poughkeepsie, New York, in 1817. (By chance, the word *trade* appeared under the picture of William and the word *mark* under that of Andrew. Thus it happened by a mere coincidence that the famous Smith Brothers trademark was born and the Smith brothers became known to generations of Americans as Trade and Mark.)

William and Andrew were the sons of James Smith, who moved to Poughkeepsie from St. Armand, Quebec, in 1817 to establish a restaurant. Though James was a fine carpenter by trade, he was an even better candy maker and businessman.

The story of the birth of the first cough drop goes like this. A journeyman stopped at the Smith restaurant and gave James the formula for a delicate and effective cough candy. James saw a need for such a product in the cold, windswept Hudson Valley and immediately mixed up a batch on his kitchen stove. The drops were a quick success, and demand for the "cough candy" grew fast up and down the river. In 1852, the firm's first advertisement appeared in the Poughkeepsie newspaper.

Young William and Andrew were active in the new business from the start. They helped mix the secret formula in their father's kitchen and busily sold the product in the streets of Poughkeepsie. Inheriting the fast-growing business when their father died in 1866, the brothers officially named the company Smith Brothers.

Phil Knight, Nike

The Nike athletic machine began as a small distributing outfit located in the trunk of Phil Knight's car. From these rather inauspicious beginnings, Knight's brainchild grew to become the shoe and athletic company that would come to define many aspects of popular culture and myriad varieties of "cool."

Nike originated from two sources: coach Bill Bowerman's quest for lighter, more durable racing shoes for his Oregon runners, and Knight's search for a way to make a living without having to give up his love of athletics. Bowerman coached track at the University of Oregon, where Phil Knight ran in 1959. Bowerman's desire for better-quality running shoes clearly influenced Knight in his search for a marketing strategy. Between them, the seed of the most influential sporting company grew.

While getting his M.B.A. at Stanford University, Knight took a class with Frank Shallenberger. The semester-long project was to devise a small business, including a marketing plan. Synthesizing Bowerman's attention to quality running shoes and the burgeoning opinion that high-quality/low-cost products could be produced in Japan and shipped to the United States for distribution, Knight found his market niche. Shallenberger thought the idea interesting but certainly no business jackpot. Knight's project was shelved.

In 1963, Phil Knight traveled to Japan on a world tour. On a whim, he scheduled an interview with a Japanese running shoe manufacturer, Tiger. Presenting himself as the representative of an American distributor interested in selling Tiger shoes to American runners, Knight told the businesspeople of his interest in their product. Blue Ribbon Sports was born. The Tiger execs liked what they heard, and Knight placed his first order for Tigers shortly thereafter.

By the following year, Knight had sold $8,000 worth of Tigers and placed an order for more. In 1971, after crediting $1 million in sales and riding the wave of the success, Knight and his associates created the Nike name and trademark swoosh. By the late 1970s, Blue Ribbon Sports had officially become Nike and had gone from $10 million to $270 million in sales. For the quarter ending in February 2006, the company's net income grew to $325.8 million.

And it all started in the back of a car.

Steve Wozniak, Apple Computer

Known as the Wizard of Woz, Steve Wozniak (along with Steve Jobs) founded Apple Computers and started a computer revolution that has never slowed down. As a child, Wozniak was enthralled with mathematics and computers. He often became so engrossed in those worlds that his mother would have to physically shake him back to reality. This love of mathematics drove Wozniak's childhood ambition to seek a career as an engineer.

Wozniak and Jobs designed what would be the Apple I in Jobs's bedroom, and they built the prototype in Jobs's garage. Jobs was able to convince a local electronic retailer to order twenty-five Apple Is. In order to raise the capital needed to make these machines, Jobs and Wozniak had to sell their most valuable possessions—Jobs's Volkswagen microbus and Wozniak's Hewlett-Packard scientific calculator. This enabled them to raise $1,300. With that base capital and credit begged from local electronics suppliers, they set up their first product line.

Needless to say, the company has continued to grow by leaps and bounds. For the fiscal quarter ending in June 2006, Apple posted revenue of $4.37 billion and a net quarterly profit of $472 million.

David Packard, Hewlett-Packard

David Packard, an attorney's son, was born and raised in Pueblo, Colorado, where he became the secretary of the local amateur radio club at the age of twelve. Fred Terman's textbook on radio engineering helped to lure Packard to Stanford University, where, like Bill Hewlett, he became one of Terman's prize students.

After graduation, Packard worked for General Electric in the East for a short time before returning to Stanford to earn a graduate degree in engineering. Packard and his wife, Lucile, provided the humble garage where the company began. Here the partners built audio oscillators for the Disney film *Fantasia* as their first big contract.

Debbi Fields, Mrs. Fields Cookies

How did Debbi Fields, a young homemaker barely out of her teens, manage to create the huge cookie store empire called Mrs. Fields Cookies? In short, by sticking to her beliefs and following her own heart. Today the Mrs. Fields Cookies empire consists of more than one thousand company-owned and franchised stores in the United States and eight foreign countries.

Fields actually got the idea to go into the cookie business when she was only ten and started to bake cookies as a hobby. At thirteen, she discovered the importance of quality. She is reported to have said, "When I made my cookies using butter for the very first time and instantly knew that butter tasted better, I was hooked on quality and was never going to compromise on quality or the ingredients I used."

Though people close to her, including her own family, told her she would fail, she refused to accept that. Virtually everyone told her that the idea of starting a store to sell chocolate chip cookies was ridiculous. Considering the fact that Fields had no start-up money, no college degree, no business experience, and no track record, it was no easy task to remain positive about her vision. But she had a dream and a recipe and eventually found a financial institution that was willing to give her a chance, and Mrs. Fields Cookies was born!

More Home-Based Success Stories

Here are some other well-known, powerful companies that began as home-based enterprises:

Avon Products
Baskin-Robbins
Brookstone
Cape Cod Potato Chips
Celestial Seasonings
Domino's Pizza

Estée Lauder Companies
Ford Motor Company
Gateway 2000
Gillette Company
Hallmark
Johnson Wax
Lane Bryant
Liquid Paper
Mary Kay Cosmetics
Microsoft
Pepperidge Farm
Reader's Digest
Russell Stover Candies
S.O.S. Pads
StairMaster
Walt Disney Company
Welch's Grape Juice

CHAPTER THREE

You as a Small-Business Owner

Whenever you see a successful business,
someone once made a courageous decision.
—Peter Drucker

When you're starting a new venture, you need to spell out all the particulars in a valuable document called a business plan. If you need to seek financial backing, your business plan is what will show potential backers whether your venture is a sound investment. The business plan will require a good deal of thought and research, so be sure to give yourself enough time to prepare it before scheduling meetings with banks or other financial backers.

Elements of a Business Plan

Although there is no one prescribed method of writing a business plan, most experts agree that you should include the following eight major elements. For additional information, see the books listed in Appendix B.

Describe Your Mission

Before you begin to write your business plan, work on constructing a mission statement. Don't feel overwhelmed by the idea! Just jot down what it is that you hope to accomplish. What is your mission and what do you want your company's mission to be? Once you've got the basic idea written, you can think more about fine-tuning it to present your mission in the clearest possible way.

Describe the Business

Write a broad definition of the business and then become more specific. It's important to keep both your broad and specific definitions in mind when your business is launched. However, you may later decide to stay in the same broad category but make some adjustments in the more specific business focus.

Describe the Products and Services

Does your dream company offer a product—such as the most efficient widget in the world—or a service—such as finding the best gifts for everyone on your clients' holiday and birthday lists? Whatever the case may be, whether you are interested in supplying the public with a product or a service, your business plan must define this. Be as specific as possible in identifying what it is you plan to market and sell.

Identify the Target Market

This area requires a great deal of research. For your business to be successful, you have to know if people have a need for your product or service and if they are willing to pay for it. Though large companies hire marketing firms to determine this, you can conduct your own research through smaller market surveys.

Ask people you know (and those you don't) if they would use your product or service and find out why or why not. If they use a similar service or have in the past, ask them what they would like to see improved. What would they be willing to pay? Survey similar businesses, both in your area and in other communities, to get an idea of the prices they charge. Then decide (based on your projected start-up costs and monthly expenses) how much you will need to charge to meet your financial objectives.

Assess the Competition

Contact your local chamber of commerce and nearest Small Business Development Center (SBDC) to learn how many businesses similar to yours exist and if they are busy. Check with county offices that deal with small businesses, advisory councils, and the Department of Labor's *Occupational Outlook Handbook* (www.bls.gov/oco) to track statistics on business growth in your area. Examine competing businesses. Do you offer something unique and possibly better?

Describe Equipment Needed to Operate

You may need office equipment such as desks, lamps, chairs, filing cabinets, computer, printer, photocopy machine, answering machine, scanner, paper goods, books, shelving units, phones, calculators, staplers, paper clips, business cards, and so forth. Take into consideration any special items your business might require—for example, age-appropriate toys for a day care business or a pickup truck if you plan to do construction work.

Summarize Your Budget

Prepare a summary of your projected start-up costs, income, and possible monthly cash flow statements for the first year.

Start-Up Expenses. Here is a sample list of expenses you might incur as you start your home business:

- Licenses, permits, and registrations
- Office equipment—computer, printer, copier, telephone, fax machine, and other electronic equipment
- Office supplies

- Office furniture—desk, table, chair, bookcase, filing cabinet
- Fixtures
- Required remodeling or redecorating
- Electrical work
- Telephone service installation
- Merchandise
- Initial promotional expenses: brochures, stationery, business cards, advertising, website
- Marketing costs—promotional events and announcements
- Internet service
- Software
- Post office box and postage (possibly a postage meter)
- Professional association dues
- Books and other resource materials
- Insurance
- Car and expenses
- Education—seminars or workshops
- Consulting fees for various professionals
- Legal and accounting fees

Though these costs may vary considerably, some experts estimate that figures can range from a few hundred dollars to $40,000 for a small business and $200,000 or more for a larger operation.

Ongoing Expenses. The following list will give you an idea about ongoing expenses you may be faced with each month.

- Independent contract fees
- Travel and auto expenses
- Supplies
- Merchandise
- Deliveries

- Cleaning and maintenance
- Insurance (medical and any applicable professional insurances required)
- Employee salary, benefits, and payroll taxes (if you hire employees)

Chart Your Course. It's an excellent idea to create a cash flow chart for at least your first year of business. Your statement should show, month by month, how much money will be coming into the business and how much will be going out. This allows you to be aware of when you will have a financial excess and when you foresee a deficit that you might have to cover. You may then have some additional time to budget so the money is available when you need it.

Summarize Your Business Goals

Be honest with yourself and list everything you hope to achieve, including both short-range and long-range objectives. Short range may include setting up your home office or applying for a loan to purchase basic equipment. Long range may include getting a certain number of customers in the first year or making a profit of a specific amount. (Bear in mind that for many small businesses, it takes two years or more before any profit is realized.)

Review your objectives daily, weekly, monthly, and yearly to see if your business is headed in the right direction. You may want to add or subtract some objectives as your business grows.

A Sample Business Plan

The following business plan should be used as an example, not a model to follow for your particular business. This is a preliminary plan, designed to get the business started. Additional information would be added on an ongoing basis.

JANGEE COMPUTER CONSULTING COMPANY

This company is in the process of being formed as a sole proprietorship owned and operated by Jan Goldberg. This business plan is being developed as a guide to beginning and managing this new business.

Mission Statement

To provide fast and reliable technical help to small office computer users. Thus, JanGee will offer technical aid and support on an hourly basis, in a retainer capacity, or by the project.

Start-Up Expenses

About $2,500 will be in the form of owner investment, which includes the cost of installing an additional phone line as well as the following:

$700 for an all-in-one printer, fax, answering machine, scanner
$250 for legal fees
$100 for stationery
$125 for brochures
$125 for an accountant
$150 for insurance
$425 rent for that area (proportioned; utilities included)

Objectives

Short-term objective: to get the company started as inexpensively as possible, incurring a minimum of debt. Long-term objective: to promote the company into a solid growth pattern so that it is a profitable enterprise that the owner can comfortably run.

Pricing Strategy

This includes an hourly figure of $75 (comparable to competitors), $150 to $200 on retainer, and a project day rate of eight hours at $75 per hour.

Keys to Success

These will lie in effective marketing and networking, quick response times, quality, guaranteed service, and the establishment of a client base of satisfied customers.

Marketing

This will include sending some basic sales literature in the form of an announcement letter and brochures to all possible contacts. The new company logo will appear on all stationery and brochures. Also, a basic Web page will be established. The owner will do all of the designing. Subsequently, there will be press releases, announcements, and other news items sent through the local media.

Competition

Though there are a fair number of competitors, customers in the area complain that many are not reliable or efficient. Also, several are more specialized and do not target small business owners. It is also important to note that the growth trend for this market is estimated at about 10 percent annually for the next decade.

Help with Your Business Plan

There are books that can help you with creating your business. Check at your library or bookstore, or visit www.amazon.com to look for appropriate titles. Appendix B includes some suggestions to get you started. You can also contact your local chamber of commerce or Small Business Development Center (SBDC), or you might even want to consider hiring a professional business consultant.

Seeking Assistance from Professionals

Seeking the assistance of a number of valuable professionals will help you to get your home-based business off to a good start. Lawyers, accountants, professional business consultants, or financial advisers usually work on an hourly basis, charging anywhere from about $100 an hour on up. Their final fees would depend upon how much of their assistance you need and how complicated your business establishment is. With each professional you consult, there are some specific considerations to keep in mind.

Legal Assistance. Try to locate a lawyer who specifically deals with small businesses. This way he or she will be aware of all the special nuances germane to starting and running a home-based small business. Particular tasks the lawyer might accomplish for you include legalizing your business name (though you may be able to do this yourself) and offering valuable information that should work toward protecting you and your business from any potential lawsuits. Because this is such an important area, you should hire someone who is specifically qualified for this role. Don't try to cut corners here!

Accounting Assistance. Finding a dependable accountant is also very important. You want to have someone who can provide all of the information you need to set up a credible accounting system. He or she should also teach you about all of the pertinent papers you need to save for tax purposes. You will most likely want to use an accountant to file your annual (and/or quarterly) taxes, so it's important to find someone you are comfortable discussing your finances with.

It is also a good idea to invest in accounting software. Although you'll still need the services of a professional accountant, a software package will make it easier to keep track of your expenses and profits. Programs such as QuickBooks allow you to track customers and inventory, prepare invoices, and generate reports.

Business and Financial Assistance. Professional business consultants or financial advisers can provide a wealth of information for you. They may aid in setting up the business, point you toward sources of start-up capital, help with the bookkeeping system, and provide insights into the operation of the business. They may also show you how to speed up, improve, or streamline your business.

Insurance Assistance. A licensed property and casualty agent is the professional you should consult for suggestions on what you should purchase in the way of business insurance. Unlike lawyers and accountants, licensed property and casualty agents don't usually charge for consultations. They receive their compensation from percentages of the policy premiums you pay. To find someone who can handle this for you, you might start with your existing homeowner's policy agent. If the agent can't handle the additional insurance needs for your business, perhaps he or she can make some suggestions of others who can.

Even if your office consists of a PC, desk, and secondhand chair, you'll want coverage in case of a minor catastrophe. Your homeowner's policy may cover you, but it may not cover your business. Even if it does, the coverage will be minimal—perhaps $2,500 for equipment and $250 for damage that occurs to goods removed from your home. At the least, you want to cover your equipment in case of fire or theft.

If you have a cell phone or laptop that you take with you on the road, you may want to secure off-premises coverage, too. Liability insurance can also be important, especially if someone slips in your office, breaks a leg, and decides to sue you.

Another option is business interruption insurance, which provides coverage in the event you are unable to operate the business for a time. One thing you cannot skip is medical insurance. Life and disability insurance are also important.

Assistance from Other Sources. In addition to seeking help from all of these professionals, you should also check out the chamber of commerce, bank, state bar association, state association of insurance agents, and local business clubs. Also, make a trip to your local library to look at the county business and professional directories. Perhaps most important of all, try to locate others who are already running their own home-based businesses, particularly in your area. These are the people with firsthand knowledge of what it's like to be involved in this kind of work. They may be able to tell you what to avoid and what to seek out.

Before hiring any experts—ask questions, ask questions, ask questions! This is an extremely important juncture in your life, so rest assured that there are no dumb questions. If you don't know the answer, it's a legitimate question, and you're most likely not the first one to ask!

Become informed about all of the issues involved and about who are the best people to help you in your quest to start and build a successful home-based business. If you hire someone and you aren't satisfied with his or her services, find someone who seems more willing and better able to serve you the way you wish to be served. It's your business—you are in charge and should feel comfortable with the people you choose to be part of your support system. If they don't add to the support, move on to others.

More Decisions to Make

As you can see, planning your own business involves many decisions. Here are two more that you should consider very carefully before finalizing your plans.

Solo or Duo?

Are you thinking of including a partner in your new business? If so, you should talk this idea over thoroughly beforehand with your lawyer, who can explain to you both the advantages and the disadvantages of a sole proprietorship (a business owned by one person) and a partnership (a business owned by two or more people). About 75 percent of all businesses are owned by one person.

The main advantage of a sole proprietorship is that you don't have to consult anyone before making a business decision. You can take your company anywhere you choose and keep all of the profits. It's also the least expensive way to set up a business in terms of registration and legal fees.

However, you also have all of the responsibilities and liabilities of the company. This means that you—and only you—must pay off all business debts and that if you can't, you may be subject to liquidation. Working as a sole proprietor, you must also be able to handle all aspects of the business. Whatever help you need, you must find.

If you have a partner, then, of course, that partner has a say (probably an equal say) in what path you'll take, who will help you, what products or services you'll offer, what hours your business will be open, and a host of other questions and issues.

Be sure that you don't enter a partnership without a legal, binding document. It should include all of the particulars of the arrangement, such as how much money each of the partners is investing, how the profit will be shared, what duties each will perform, what happens if one person wishes to sell his or her portion or dies. Any other eventualities should also be addressed. The document needs to protect all parties' interests.

Sometimes friends become partners and think they don't need a legal contract, which could be a big mistake. In the end, the partners may not remain friends because of misunderstandings in the concepts of the partnership. If everything had been spelled out in black and white, this might not have happened.

A corporation is a more complex business association in which the business becomes a legal entity in itself with powers and liabilities independent from the persons who own it. It is much more likely that your home-based business will take one of the other two forms.

The Name's the Game

It's important to decide on a business name, one that has a nice ring to it, one that carries respect. Be sure to say it out loud a number of times to see how it sounds and make sure it isn't difficult to pronounce. Even more important, make sure that it doesn't have a different meaning in another language or country—perhaps something that could be deemed unflattering. (This has actually happened!)

Before you are committed to a new name, do a prior search to make sure you aren't accidentally taking a name that is already being used by someone else. You can probably do this by simply calling the county clerk in the county where you are setting up your company. If you are launching an incorporated business, then you probably need to contact the secretary of state's office in your state to check this matter out. If your plans are to make your company a national enterprise, contact the registrar of copyrights at the Library of Congress, where you can establish a national trademark or service mark.

You may want to choose a name that uses a word or words that describe what you do. For instance, *Jan's Fabulous Cake Creations* lets you know who the owner of the company is and what the company specializes in. However, keep in mind that as your business grows and develops, you may want to go into areas you didn't originally think you would, and the name may no longer fit.

After you've settled the question of your company name, you will probably be required to publish a "Doing Business As" (DBA) announcement under "fictitious businesses" in the classified sections of one of the newspapers in your town or the court where your business is located. You will be required to list your company name, a description of your business, and the business location— which, in the case of a home-based business, would be your home address. You may also need to go through this procedure or a similar one before you can establish a bank account for your business. Laws vary from state to state, so always be sure to determine what applies in your home state by checking with your secretary of state's office.

Naming an e-Business. Choosing your domain name is very important. The most recognizable names are the .com names, but so many are already in use that it's possible the one you want is already taken. If this is the case, you can try a variation on the name. Or you can try to contact the owner of the domain and see if you can work out a deal to buy the name. If the .com version isn't available, you might try .net or .org. There are newer domain names available, like .biz, .info, and .us, but these aren't as widely recognized.

Because your domain is an important part of your business, you should be sure to protect it through a trademark. Having trademark rights allows you to protect your domain name against others who might allege that it infringes on their rights, and allows you to enforce your trademark rights against others who use domain names similar to yours to try to divert your customers.

Trademark law is very complex and is probably something that you shouldn't try to handle on your own. It would be best to consult an attorney to discuss the best possibilities for you. You can also find more information from the U.S. Patent and Trademark Office at www.uspto.gov.

Licenses, Permits, and Resale Tax Numbers

Depending on where you live and the kind of business you will be conducting, you may have to secure a license, permit, resale tax number, or all three to operate. Locally, check with your city, town, or borough as to zoning and other regulations regarding a home business. With county regulations, contact the office of your county clerk.

In most states, the business identification numbers you must get in order to conduct business include a resale tax number and a tax exemption number.

Resale Tax Number. If you sell any product to consumers, most states require you to collect sales tax. Your resale tax number is also your tax exemption number, which allows you to buy supplies wholesale without paying sales tax. Contact your state department of revenue to get a number and to obtain sales tax filing procedures.

Tax Exemption Number. If you sell products wholesale only, you do not need to collect sales tax, but you do need a tax exemption number, which also allows you to buy wholesale supplies without paying sales tax. If you sell wholesale, you must record the resale tax number of the shop that buys from you for your tax records. The Internal Revenue Service (IRS) website at www.irs.ustreas.gov offers tax information, forms, publications, and information about how to contact the IRS.

Establish a Business Bank Account

When you are ready to open for business, it's time to open a business bank account. This will keep your start-up money and income earned separate from your personal account. If your business is not a corporation, you will need a social security number or a federal employer identification number (if you plan to hire employees) from your local IRS office. If you are a sole proprietor and do not employ others, your social security number can be used as your federal identification.

Talk to other business owners in your area and ask which financial institutions they use and why. Shop around and compare the services of a number of banks and see which one best fits the needs of your business.

Write Your Job Description

Do you know what it is that you are going to have to do as the sole proprietor or partner in a new home-based business? Maybe it's a good idea for you to find out! After doing your research (through books, established business owners, and other sources), write up your job description. Remember that it's difficult to wear a large number of hats, so try to limit them as much as possible by having others help you, particularly in areas where your skills or experience are not very strong.

Prime Time

Are you considering this business as a part-time or full-time endeavor? People often begin their businesses on a part-time basis while they are employed by someone else full-time. This way, they have the stability of a full-time salary in addition to health benefits and other important compensations. Once the business gets going and seems firmly planted, they quit their full-time jobs to engage in their home-based businesses on a full-time basis.

Whether you begin your business as a part- or full-time venture, you should think of launching it on a small scale and then expanding from there. Many businesses fail because they start too large or expand too quickly. Be careful.

Managing Your Time

No matter how much time you are able to put into your new business, it won't seem like enough. There is always more to do. Owning your own business involves so many aspects—marketing and advertising, merchandising, pricing, bookkeeping, locating customers—that you can always be doing something more to try to increase your revenues from the business.

So that brings us to the important issue of time management, something most of us are perennially trying to master. In fact, the topic is so common that there are countless books and tapes available, which many people find very helpful. Check some out! The listings in Appendix B provide a great start.

Tips for Time Management

Here are some time-management tips to help you work effectively in your home-based business.

- **Establish your priorities.** Figure out what really is the most important thing that you need to get done and tackle that first!
- **Set your goals.** Write down what it is that you hope to accomplish and then keep the list handy so that you will always be reminded of your goals.
- **Don't deceive yourself.** Keep your feet firmly planted on the ground. Don't think you can accomplish goals that are totally unrealistic.
- **Get organized.** Those who are organized waste a minimum amount of time on all tasks. They don't have to look for papers, books, references, sources, or any other information before they get started on projects. Things are in logical places, aptly separated, and marked for future reference. Not only do you need to organize your things, you need to organize your workday. Here are several ways to accomplish this: You can set up your day according to your work demands, the times of the day that you are most productive, other priorities in your life, specific work tasks, or what you feel like tackling first—but be careful, you might never get to the things you don't feel like doing!
- **Make it bite size.** Some projects are so large that they seem overwhelming. If you can somehow break them down into bite-size pieces, you will feel much more capable of dealing successfully with them. Sit down with pen and paper in

hand and think about how you can break the large project into smaller sections. Not only will the job seem much more palatable and doable, but you can also reward yourself when you have completed each of the bite-size pieces along the way.

Tips for Working Efficiently

Procrastination can be a deadly drain on the success of your home-based business. Get down to work and stick to business! When you do so, reward yourself and enjoy the reward. Avoid interruptions—let the phone ring or have your answering device take care of it and don't answer the door (unless you're expecting someone important).

Plan your day and always set deadlines to complete projects, parts of projects, and tasks. Cross off what you have finished and congratulate and reward yourself. Praise yourself for a job well done. Take short breaks frequently.

A change of scenery is always a good idea. If possible, collect your present project and take it with you over to a local bookstore, café, or restaurant. The number of establishments that offer Internet access make it easy for you to bring your laptop and get some work done. This is a good way to rejuvenate yourself and ward off that "cooped up" feeling. It is also a good stress reliever.

Here are some other good ways to help reduce the sense of isolation:

- Join professional associations and organizations
- Make a concerted effort to keep in touch with people you have worked with previously—especially ones who are still working in your same field
- Volunteer
- Enroll in some classes
- Attend workshops and seminars
- Arrange face-to-face meetings with clients or potential clients

Marketing Your New Business

To a great extent, the success of your business will depend on your ability to market and advertise your products or services. You will need to promote your business whenever and wherever you can. Promotion is, essentially, communication. The better you are able to communicate to your prospective customers, the more business you will receive.

Business promotion falls into two main categories—paid and free. Paid promotion (or advertising) includes classified and display ads in newspapers, magazines, and other print media; radio and television (network and cable) ads; promotional ads such as advertisement on vehicles or pencils; business cards; telephone directories; and direct mailings. Next to equipment, paid advertising can be the biggest expense of a new business.

In marketing your new business, you must find and focus on your likely audience. Decide what the best way might be to reach those customers. You can rent (or buy or create) a list and do a direct mailing. You can compose a sales letter that includes a response card. You can try marketing at trade shows. You can offer incentives to new customers. You can try telemarketing. You can ask for referrals.

To reach a broader audience, you can place ads in the newspapers and in trade magazines. You can use signs. You can list yourself in the Yellow Pages. You can do the same in trade directories. You can even try local television or radio ads.

Free promotion or advertising includes public talks and appearances, press releases, feature articles in local newspapers, demonstrations, promotional events, or donations of your services to fund-raising auctions.

You can also look into creating free publicity through articles that local readers (and editors) will find interesting. Pitch a story to them that has local appeal.

You can (and certainly should) network, network, network. Catch the media's attention in some way. Offer your talent and expertise in the form of teaching a class, doing a presentation, or serving as an interviewed expert for an article.

Editors will more likely print your press release or follow up with a feature article if you stick to the proper format. (Check sources in your library on how to write press releases.) A press release must be neatly typed, double spaced, concise, and written on your business stationery. You might also want to include a black-and-white photograph of you conducting business. Don't forget to include the basics of news stories—who, what, when, where, why, and how. Make sure the answers to these questions appear in the first couple of paragraphs of your release. Don't forget to include how people can reach you for more information about your business.

Internet Marketing

The Internet also offers several tools for marketing your business. Many of these are free or relatively inexpensive and are worth considering as a means of maximizing your exposure to potential clients. People looking for the services you offer might use a search engine to find providers. Search engine marketing is usually done through use of a software package that include such features as search engine optimizer, search engine submitter, ranking reporter, submission scheduler, page generator, upload manager, and traffic analyzer, among others. Keyword marketing employs search engine tools that help you focus on using the right keywords to enhance your site's search engine position.

E-mail marketing is another useful Internet tool that basically involves sending bulk e-mail messages to prospective customers. Many companies offer e-mail marketing services for a fee. Pay-per-click advertising is a growing trend in Internet marketing. Using this method, your website is listed among the top results rankings in search engine queries, and you pay a set fee for every visitor to your site. Many business owners believe it is worth the relatively small investment to have a prominent listing, since most people visit only the first few sites returned in a search.

Your Choices

As you see, you can promote your business through word-of-mouth advertising, community bulletin boards, arranging to have a happening or special event, becoming a speaker at a seminar, or donating something to a charitable event.

Once you have explored your options for marketing, set a budget and decide what method of marketing you wish to use and can afford. Keep track of the effectiveness of the method you chose so that you can determine whether you should stick with it or try something else. See Appendix B for helpful books on marketing and promotions.

CHAPTER FOUR

Home-Based Franchises, Freelancers, and Consultants

In the end, all business operations can be reduced to three words: people, product, and profits. People come first.
—Lee Iacocca

Franchises, freelancing, and consulting are three excellent opportunities for those who want to start a home-based business. Each option has its own appeal for different types of homebodies.

Franchises

If the thought of launching a business of your own from scratch feels a bit too risky for your taste, you might consider looking into the idea of purchasing a franchise. If this concept appeals to you, you should associate yourself with a company that already has a strong track record of success and that will teach you how to use its proven techniques.

Today, there are more than fifteen hundred franchise brands available with over three hundred thousand individual franchise units. Because the fastest-growing segments of franchising are oriented toward service offerings, many of them can easily be run from home. In fact, the lower overhead of working from home makes the idea of running a franchise even more attractive. Another plus for owning a franchise is the fact that fewer franchises go out of business than do start-up companies.

The World of Franchises

What you are actually doing when you purchase a franchise is paying the franchiser for permission to use his or her trade name, trademark, products, and business systems. In exchange, you pay an initial fee and (usually) an ongoing royalty percentage based on your earnings from the franchise. You may also be responsible for paying some advertising fees.

One option that avoids the high costs of complying with franchising registration laws involves a license arrangement instead of a franchise. A license gives the start-up businessperson permission to use trademarks, proprietary methods, and materials. Know-how and training are also provided in exchange for a fee, and you still pay ongoing costs for goods or materials.

Franchise Bound

There are some clear advantages to buying a franchise over starting your own business. When you purchase a franchise, you are buying a tested and proven business. You'll receive training and support from the franchiser and other franchisees. Ideally, name recognition helps you automatically establish a clientele.

Also, you'll be learning about the ins and outs of the business much more quickly—a fact that should greatly shorten the amount of time before you begin to make a profit. Although you are on your own as a franchise owner, you are not alone. With a good franchise, you get the benefit of valuable business training and a great deal of support. You have access to manuals with step-by-step instructions on procedures that have already proven to be successful.

In some cases, franchisers will even provide financing for start-up fees and costs, needed equipment, required software, and promotional materials. Some also offer the benefits inherent in a national advertising campaign (or you may be responsible for some shared advertising costs). As an added bonus for the future, if you do well in your business, you can often sell it more easily than you can a sole proprietorship. The potential new owners will be able to build on your experience and the franchise name to help them get started.

This opens up the topic of another option—buying a successfully established franchise. This type of arrangement has several added advantages. You would immediately have an established cash flow. You can avoid the uncertainty of trying to project how much you could potentially make by having your accountant examine the books to determine the financial situation of the franchise. This means that much of the guesswork of starting a business is withdrawn from the equation.

Whether you decide to purchase a new or existing franchise, the help that you receive can dramatically make a difference in the amount of time and effort you need to put into getting your business up and running.

Other Realities of Owning a Franchise

Starting a home-based franchise isn't without its challenges. With the costs involved, you are probably going to have to assume some initial debt in order to make the purchase. It's important here to be careful that you don't pay a higher price than the franchise is worth. This may be especially true if the business is really a small one and the possible amount of the franchise royalty is high. Sometimes the prices of franchises are simply too high, elevated strictly on the basis of the new owner gaining name recognition. It may well be that the name isn't familiar enough to warrant such an inflated figure.

Often low start-up fees indicate that the parent company isn't capable of—or interested in—providing the support and training you seek and perhaps desperately need. It is not at all uncommon to hear about lawsuits that have been launched by franchisees (against their franchisers) for not following through with promises of support and advertising.

Another important point that has been made about franchises is that, technically speaking, a franchise is not something you actually own. And, in a strict sense, this is often true. Usually what you have purchased is a contract that allows you to operate that particular franchise for a specific period of time—perhaps ten years. At the end of that period of time, the contract may or may not be renewed. If it isn't renewed, you can no longer operate that franchise.

Do the Research

Just as is the case with any major decision—business or otherwise—purchasing a franchise is not something that should be done without a great deal of research and study. Ask as many people as you can—both professionals and potential clients—about any input they may have in the equation. Franchising is not something you should jump into on an impulse.

When considering whether to purchase a franchise, many people begin their research on the Internet. Searching the Web is a good way to learn about company histories, franchise locations, and revenue statistics. In recent years, it has become more common for people to hire franchise consultants to help them find the most appropriate franchise to purchase.

The International Franchise Association (IFA) offers a free online database of over one thousand franchises, which you can search by industry or investment required. The IFA also offers a free online course in franchising basics, as well as a link to the Federal Trade Commission's "Consumer Guide to Buying a Franchise." Visit the IFA at www.franchise.org for a wealth of information about franchise possibilities.

Questions for the Franchisers. While you are doing your research, keep in mind what you need to know in order to ask the right questions. Here are some of the important questions that you should be prepared to ask the franchisers.

1. What is the cost of the franchise?
2. What, if any, is the ongoing royalty fee?
3. What, if any, are the costs of advertising?
4. Must supplies be purchased only from the franchiser?
5. Based on my initial investment, what rate of return can I expect?
6. When should I expect to reach my break-even point?
7. What other costs are involved in operating the franchise?
8. What is a typical day in the business really like?
9. What kind of support can I expect from the franchiser?
10. Can I expect that the franchiser will be regularly available to address my questions and concerns?
11. What kind of ongoing training for owners, managers, and employees is available?
12. What is the duration of the franchise contract?
13. What are the procedures for renewing the contract?
14. How easy—or how difficult—is it to acquire the renewal of a franchise contract?
15. What possible circumstances could there be for the franchiser to ask me to leave or for me to ask to leave the system?
16. Is the home office in competition with me for business?
17. What is the company's long-range plan?
18. What is the operating yearly advertising budget and what role do I play in this?
19. What is the franchiser's mission statement?
20. How long has the company been in business?
21. How many franchises does it have?

22. Is the product or service guaranteed?
23. What is the franchiser's credit rating or cash position?
24. Will I be obtaining an exclusive territory?
25. Can my contract be sold or transferred?
26. Does the company offer any financing assistance?
27. What standards does the company use to screen applicants?
28. Is the company registered in my state?
29. Are there any pending lawsuits from franchisees or customers?

A Plethora of Possibilities

There is a wide variety of franchise categories that you could operate from home. The following list represents some of the possibilities. Start-up fees may range from nothing to $50,000.

- Answering service
- Business consulting
- Cleaning service
- Computer classes for children
- Computer consulting
- Dance classes for preschoolers
- Direct-mail advertising
- Education for children
- Executive search
- Financial planning
- Interior decorating
- Kitchen remodeling
- Lawn-care service
- Laminated children's identification tags
- Management training
- Medical claims processing
- Odd jobs service
- Parent education
- Payroll services

- Pet sitting
- Prenatal education
- Real estate advertising
- Sales training
- Skin-care products
- Tax preparation
- Upholstery cleaning
- Wedding planning
- Window cleaning service
- Windshield repair
- Video photography service
- Video repair
- Waterproofing

Freelancing

The word *freelancer* dates all the way back to the Middle Ages and refers to mercenary soldiers or military adventurers, often of knightly rank, who offered their services to any state, party, or cause. So, too, freelancers offer their services to those who need them.

The Freelance Life

Freelancers are self-employed individuals who work on their own projects and take assignments from employers as they choose. They hire out their expertise on a project basis. Clients provide freelancers with short-term assignments sealed with contracts that spell out the terms of the projects—what the freelancers will be expected to do and how they'll be paid. This could be on an hourly basis, a commission basis, or a per-project basis.

Companies that use the services of freelancers assume that they will be able to complete the assignment with little or no supervision, so home-based operations are perfect for this type of work.

Though it is possible for freelancers to work strictly for one company, usually they work for a number of companies, organizations, or agencies at the same time. Thus, they need to learn how to be efficient jugglers as they are often juggling many projects—in differing stages—at the same time.

Freelancers are responsible for cultivating and building their own client bases. Clients are often found through professional networking events, concerted marketing efforts, and word of mouth.

Freelancers must be very independent individuals, able to manage their own time and prioritize their work without anyone looking over their shoulders and telling them what to do. When potential freelance assignments come in, freelancers need to be able to assess the time it will take to complete the project so that they can schedule that time around all of their other current or potential assignments.

Depending on their backgrounds and areas of expertise, freelancers may specialize in a single category or they may take on a wide variety of types of projects.

Advantages and Disadvantages of Freelancing

There are many advantages and disadvantages of operating as a freelancer. On the plus side:

- You can set your own hours.
- You can work at home (or anywhere else, for that matter).
- Whatever you presently have in your wardrobe is all you need (although you may occasionally need to meet with clients in person and dress appropriately for those meetings).
- You are your own boss.
- Your home office or work area is yours to design any way you wish.

- You get to choose the clients you work with.
- You determine what kinds of projects you wish to work on.
- You have the freedom to take on as many or as few projects as you wish.
- You establish your own fees.

On the negative side:

- Cash flow may be erratic (or nonexistent at times).
- Sometimes you are not even promised payment until an assignment is completed or accepted as meeting the client's needs.
- Work may be scarce at times.
- Clients don't always pay when they should.
- You may feel quite isolated.
- You don't get the stimulation of working with a staff of other creative individuals.
- You usually receive no company benefits—vacation days, sick days, pension plans, medical insurance, and so forth. This is a great area of concern to many freelancers and consultants.

Despite all the advantages and disadvantages, one thing is certain. You shouldn't think of doing this on a full-time basis until you have built up a clientele or have laid the groundwork with potential clients who are close to committing projects to you. When does a potential freelancer get to the point when he or she can realistically consider doing this full-time? This is a difficult question to answer, because several things need to be taken into consideration. How much money do you need to live on? How many clients can you count on? (You'll never know this for sure, but you can estimate.) How much work will you be getting from these clients? How much money does this amount to? Where there is any doubt, the old adage about keeping your day job applies here. The stories of overnight success are just that—stories. A lot of hard work, talent, and perseverance are necessary for any real amount of success as a freelancer.

Consulting

Consulting has much in common with freelancing, yet there are distinct differences. In many cases, consultants work for only one company and are asked to (and expected to) travel, which is usually not the case for freelancers.

In both cases, the initial investment is minimal, you can set your own hours—and sometimes even hire employees—and perhaps earn a good living. Freelancers and consultants are perfect for our new economy, where staffs are trim and additional personnel are called in when there is a specific need on a particular project. After that project is completed, you are no longer on the payroll until the next project comes up or when the company needs additional help. In this way, companies can keep their payrolls as small as possible and save the costs involved in paying out benefits and full-time salaries.

Both freelancers and consultants should always be on the lookout for assignments. Even so, there may be dry spells that will send you on a roller-coaster ride of anxiety. Another negative to these careers is that you are not really a part of something bigger, like a company. You are basically on your own. Another drawback is the reality that both freelancers and consultants may be forced to work incredibly long hours to meet their deadlines for projects.

Choosing Clients

It's important for freelancers and consultants to be careful about the clients they choose to take on. One advantage they have over their salaried counterparts is that if they do make bad choices (and the client and/or project turns out to be a nightmare), they usually have only to finish that project and then they can happily drop the client from their current list (one hopes without too great a financial loss).

Important Qualities for Freelancers and Consultants

To be successful as a freelancer or consultant, you must really be proficient in sales and marketing—indeed, you will be marketing yourself whenever and wherever you can and selling yourself over and over again. After all, what people are buying is not a tangible product that can be seen, scrutinized, measured, and examined like a new car. What you are selling are your talents and your ability to do an outstanding job.

Other important qualities include a high intellect, strong interpersonal skills, honesty, energy, managerial abilities, and leadership capacities. You need to be a self-starter, one who can develop and follow a plan, stick to goals, manage time, and keep to a regular schedule of achievement. You need to be a good communicator, one who can interact well with all kinds of people.

Freelancing truly requires a great deal of flexibility—the kind required for you to identify and deal with your own strengths and weaknesses, your own assets and liabilities, to survive the ups and downs of too much or not enough work, to work well with people with all kinds of differing personalities and business outlooks who are (or will become) your customers and clients. If you possess this kind of flexibility, you can enjoy the freedom that comes with it by setting your own pace even though bombarded by a number of competing and important demands.

Freelancers and consultants must always be ready to handle a great deal of responsibility because the fact is, there's no one else who's going to handle it, so the responsibilities—and the rewards—are always theirs!

CHAPTER FIVE

Homebodies Who Offer a Product

A company is judged by the president it keeps.
—James Hulbert

The products that homebodies offer run the gamut from cookies to cleaners, from educational products to cosmetics, from books to sweaters. Featured in this chapter is a sampling of homebodies who offer their own special products. Note that while their backgrounds, training, and the way they came to start their businesses may be quite varied, they all held the belief that their dreams of successful self-employment lay in offering a product that would benefit others.

Products Sold from Home
Read the following accounts of several homebodies who have created successful businesses to see what ideas you might develop.

Julie Aigner-Clark, Founder, Baby Einstein
Julie Aigner-Clark is the founder of the Baby Einstein Company (www.babyeinstein.com), an enterprise that produces educational videos for babies. She has a bachelor of arts degree in English and psychology, as well as a teaching credential.

Julie taught for five years, until she left the profession in 1994 to raise her daughter. She found parenthood inspiring and coupled that inspiration with a commitment to see that her child flourished in every possible way—physically, intellectually, emotionally, and developmentally. This led Julie to an interest in child development, particularly in the areas of intelligence and natural awareness. She began to research these fields and was surprised to find that nothing was available in the area of language acquisition for infants. Julie decided to create her own product, laying the foundation for the Baby Einstein Company.

While getting the business off the ground, Julie's main commitment was still her children. Running the business and planning her workday revolved around their schedules. With one child in preschool five mornings a week, Julie used her baby's naptime during those mornings to return calls, handle correspondence, and complete agreements. She also hired three assistants who worked out of her house, answering calls, processing orders, shipping, and maintaining the house.

In the early days of the business, prioritizing was very important to Julie. "I used to try to do everything myself, and I went insane!" she says. "There's way too much for one person to handle and handle well. It meant sitting down and thinking about what was the most important thing to me. Family—without a doubt." With this in mind, she decided to work around the children's schedules and found a way to make this work. As she says, "My kids are only going to be little for a short time, and I want to be there for them and give them the best of life that I can, while I can."

Julie believes in what she does and is proud of the products she has created. Frequent positive feedback from parents provides a real boost and helps her to appreciate the excitement of creating a successful product.

Julie says that she is not naturally business oriented, so figuring out the business end of things was not always easy and has been her least favorite part of the work. Establishing the business was a learning process, with mistakes along the way. While some mistakes were costly, everything has paid off in the end. In 2001 the Baby Einstein Company was acquired by the Walt Disney Company and now includes music and video products, toys, books, and clothing.

When asked what advice she would give to anyone considering starting a similar company, she says, "I would tell others who might be thinking of creating a company like mine to believe in your ideas! And if you want to work at home with small children, get help. It's difficult to find a balance, and a little baby doesn't (and shouldn't have to) understand the concept of waiting quietly. Remember the important things in life. You can always go back to work, but you can never go back to those moments when your child takes her first steps."

Debra Moss, Photographer

"I always enjoyed photography as a hobby," says Debra Moss, a Florida freelance photographer and writer, "so I decided to turn it into a career. I worked as a freelance contract archeologist surveyor for five years in Florida, Georgia, and the U.S. Virgin Islands after receiving my master of arts degree in archeology from Ohio State University in Columbus. In 1987, I became a freelance photographer while living in the Virgin Islands. I covered Caribbean travel, yachting, and sailing regattas.

"Then I began searching for a way to add creativity and soul to my life, so I built a portfolio and started sending it out to magazines, hoping to sell my work. Several editors called me and said they loved my photos, but could I write something to go with them? I have always loved writing, so I gave it a shot. Soon I was specializing in selling text/photo packages to magazines. I now have more than 150 published credits, including some very well-respected ones such as *Outside*, *Bicycling*, *Yachting*, and many others. I penned columns on computer use for writers, historical and architectural photography, and how to shoot sailboat races and other action sports. I was the press liaison for the internationally known America's Paradise Triathlon on St. Croix.

"My technique is somewhat unique—I use only natural light and have never owned a flash system, so all my work is done outdoors. I try to capture only beauty and have never gone in for what I call the somber side of the profession, photography noir.

"Travel photography, in particular, has allowed me to travel to many places on a magazine's budget. This has probably been the greatest lure. For example, this past March a magazine sent me to Costa Rica to shoot and write an article on surfing. Since I am a surfer, this was quite an enticing offer—and much fun. I love my work, and people are always stunned by the way my camera sees things.

"I took a creative writing class once, but I have no formal education in [writing], nor have I ever even taken a photography course. I am told I have 'an eye,' which I believe is an innate ability to see the world in a specific way. (I learned this from a famous photographer who looked at my work and said exactly that— 'Well, you certainly have the eye.') After that, it's mostly a matter of learning the mechanics of light, shutters, and lenses—the tools of the trade.

"In six years of college, I learned that anything you could ever want to know is in books, so I read every photography book that I could find, and then went out and shot a hundred rolls of film. That was the sum total of my training.

"Every day is a completely new experience. I don't photograph every day because I work on assignment, but I do write every day. I occasionally go out and shoot for fun so as not to lose sight of the joy I used to feel when I did it only for me and not a paying customer. My husband works at night, and I only shoot in the day, so sometimes he comes with me and carries my equipment. He is not taken in by the art of what I do particularly, but he enjoys watching me work and going to the places it takes me. I am now living near the ocean outside Jacksonville, Florida, and have done numerous articles and photos on Amelia Island for *Ritz Carlton* magazine.

"In a normal week, I work about five hours a day, five days a week. The rest of the time I train for triathlons and surf. Not a bad life.

"What bothered me most at first was my insecurity. I hadn't proven to myself that I had earned the right to represent myself as 'a photographer.' My first assignment was scary, as I was expected to produce what someone else wanted, and what if I couldn't, or my camera broke, or it rained? It was nerve-wracking, and I don't like stress much, but over the years I have learned what I can do, what I am pretty good at, and what I can do that hardly anyone else can. That self-knowledge of specialty has taken the stress away.

"Also, the uncertainty of payment when you freelance almost requires you have a steady backup income (a spouse or trust fund is nice) or at least a nest egg so that you can go for six months without seeing a dime to get you through until that blissful day when ten [payments] arrive in the mail together. Other than that, I think being a photographer is just about the neatest profession there is.

"I would recommend that you read everything there is to read, take your camera everywhere you go, and let your camera take you places you would never have gone."

Bob Mander, Print Production Worker and Author

Bob Mander earned a bachelor of arts degree in languages from Eastern Illinois University in Charleston, Illinois. Today he serves as president of his own company, Ryan and Company of Chicago. Beginning his career at United Press International (UPI) as a news reporter, Bob progressed through editorial positions in trade publications to corporate and association media to director of communications at the American College of Obstetricians and Gynecologists.

Bob left the corporate world in 1982 and entered sales as a representative for a commercial printer. Seven years later, he established his own company, specializing in high-quality corporate printing. Changes in the industry led to a reconfiguration of the company in 1999, which called for a focus on services to the publishing profession. He is the author of *Sales: Building Lifetime Skills for Success*.

In 1997 Bob began working on a prototype of his book for a business magazine, and it was during this time that he actually began formulating the concepts to adapt his business. Working on the articles made him realize that many people need to develop sales skills, but none more so than entrepreneurs. Bob's background in print production was a great help, and as he worked on his book he also learned about publishing and built a growing list of contacts, both for vendor support and potential customers.

Bob fully enjoys all aspects of his business, which requires a special set of skills that creates its own unique selling proposition. He is familiar with writing, marketing, editing, graphics, printing, publishing, and distribution. This combination of skills and experience enables him to help new authors and small publishers gain exposure and earn income.

Bob says, "It sometimes seems that my whole career has led me to this business. I can't take credit for planning it this way—it just seemed to happen, with a little push from a radically changing world. As the industries and professions I worked in gradually became obsolete or commoditized or too bureaucratic due to mergers and acquisitions, I learned to adapt. Back in the 1960s, Marshall McLuhan said, "In the electronic age, no one should be the same person or stay in the same occupation for more than ten years." Now even ten years seems excessive. The hard part is the need to constantly mess with your identity. I am an author or I am a printer or I am a marketing expert. Those are specialized and segmented concepts left over from the Industrial Age. The computer tends to integrate everything. I guess I think of myself as an Electronic Age Benjamin Franklin."

Bob enjoys the productive aspects of his work, whether this involves giving a successful interview or filling orders in a timely fashion. He also finds anticipating and dealing with problems satisfying, but dislikes the bureaucratic aspects of business, such as taxes.

One of the things he likes most about his job is the variety and not having a typical workday. One day he might give an interview to a newspaper and appear on television or at a book signing. The next day might include a press check or working on a production schedule.

"It's definitely whole-brain work," he says, "requiring both the spontaneous right brain and the analytical skills of the left brain. Public appearances and customer work require fast thinking and performance skills, while the production aspects require a hard, intense focus on detail and sequencing. You just hope you don't have to switch horses too often in the course of a single day. But even this becomes easier with practice. It's not dangerous in the physical sense, of course, but slipping out of character can lead to disaster. How many hours a week? Who counts?"

When asked about what advice he would give to anyone interested in starting a similar business, Bob cites experience as the key. "There's nothing I do that thirty years of experience won't enable anyone to do," he says. "Perhaps that might sound harsh to young people just starting out. But we hear so much today about six-month wonders who become overnight billionaires that I think it needs saying."

In addition, Bob advises doing something that you love and can excel at. He stresses the need for persistence and flexibility, as well as the importance of continuing to learn and redefine yourself to create value in your market.

Carol Revzan, Weaver and Yarn Business Owner

Carol Revzan has loved to make things since her grandmother taught her to knit and crochet many years ago. After several years of practicing these two crafts, she also learned to weave. Today she is a weaver and owns a yarn business in Evanston, Illinois.

Carol is fascinated by the practice of manipulating a strand of yarn into fabric or clothing. The limitless combinations of color, texture, and weave structures ensure that she will never be at a loss for a project; in fact, for the last forty years Carol has never been without a project involving yarn. She also loves selling yarn and helping customers find just what they need for their own projects.

Carol has a studio in her home and works there alone. She usually starts working at 9 A.M. and weaves until noon, then continues after lunch. Later in the afternoon, she works on finishing past projects or planning new ones. She devotes a good deal of time to designing and planning a project before working with yarn on the loom. Carol also hosts monthly weaving classes and always makes time for customers who come by to purchase yarn.

What Carol enjoys most about working from home is having the freedom to set her own schedule. She can develop designs and projects as she wishes and still make the time to continue to learn. On the negative side, the work is sometimes lonely. It is also difficult to get a large financial return for the time and effort that she puts into her handwoven items.

Carol's advice for others is this: "I would tell others that good weaving techniques are essential and that a background in color theory and art are most helpful. Though it's difficult to make a living at it, combined with other activities it can be very rewarding."

Sara Gast, Floral Designer

Sara Gast is a self-employed floral designer in Bloomington, New York. She received her bachelor of fine arts in ceramics from State University of New York at New Paltz. After working as a floral designer at Mohonk Mountain House in New Paltz for a few years, she decided to work as a freelance floral designer.

Sara worked as a potter for a time, but after burning out, she decided that she wanted to work with plants. She found that she excelled at floral design, due in part to the potential it presents to combine three things that she loves—working with plants, gardening, and creating artwork.

Sara credits her first floral design at Mohonk Mountain House with teaching her a great deal about the craft. She even won a Best of Show award at the International Flower Show, which included a trip to Holland.

In her current business, Sara works mainly on weddings and parties. She has one employee with whom she creates all the floral designs for weddings, including arrangements for the bridal party, decorations for the church, centerpieces, buffet displays, and cake decorations. At times Sara doesn't have any work, and other times she's swamped. When she is setting up a job, things are very busy. On some weekends, Sara has three or four events to handle, which will involve working full-time, from 9 A.M. to 5 P.M., for as many days as it takes to get the job done. Her workweek begins on Wednesday with a 4 A.M. visit to the flower market in New York City, a two-hour drive from Bloomington.

Sara loves being her own boss. She can take only those jobs that she wants, work with and for people she likes, and get paid to create art. And one of the nicest perks is the compliments she receives for her designs. She puts pressure on herself to make her designs as perfect as possible but says that the work atmosphere is usually pleasant.

The downside is the sporadic nature of the work—sometimes there is no work for long periods, followed by a deluge of projects. While Sara would prefer having a more regular schedule of events, she knows that it just isn't possible.

To anyone considering a home-based career in floral design, Sara says, "I would advise those considering flower design to live in an area where there is a demand for what you do and not a glut of others already doing it. In any case, it is not a way to get rich. I do it mostly because I love it, and I find it a challenge to realize someone's dream of what they want. So far, so good!"

Home-Based Businesses Offering a Product

In this chapter, we've seen that virtually any product that you believe in can become the center of your home-based business. Whether you have an affinity for developing an educational product, as Julie Aigner-Clark had, or turning a hobby into a career, as Debra Moss did, or enjoy commercial printing, as Bob Mander does, or are artistically inclined, like Carol Revzan and Sara Gast, the choices are yours to make, and the possibilities are endless!

CHAPTER SIX

Homebodies Who Offer a Service

Boldness in business is the first, second, and third thing.
—Thomas Fuller

As busy as everyone is these days, companies offering a service can be in high demand. Great numbers of people are willing to spend substantial amounts of money to receive the benefits of a worthwhile service.

This chapter profiles a number of individuals who have chosen to take advantage of our fast-paced modern society by offering a service through their home-based businesses. These people present only a small sampling of the wide variety of possibilities that exist for service-oriented companies. Just think about any task you perform—either on a consistent or an occasional basis—and chances are you could develop a business based upon this chore. Food for thought!

Services Offered from Home

The following accounts cover a range of services. Keep reading to learn how these homebodies fulfilled their dreams to start successful businesses.

Susan Sheehan, Website Consultant

Susan Sheehan's home-based business is Starfish Design, which handles website consultation, design, and management. The way she started her company eight years ago is inspiring for other hopeful entrepreneurs.

Susan wanted to stay at home with her children and needed a job that she could do on her own time. As the former owner and manager of two flower shops, she felt that she had gained enough business experience to strike out on her own. She was comfortable with computers and interested in a challenge. Web design seemed to fit the bill.

"Initially, I bought a fifteen-hundred-page book on Web design, sat down, read the entire book, and proceeded to set up a personal website," Susan says. "I then called a friend who had a huge website professionally designed and told her I could do it better for 10 percent less money. I got the job, and the rest followed from there!"

When Susan started her business, Web design was a new field and there were no classes available, but she did take classes in computer science and had a basic interest in design. This combination, plus her business experience, gave her the knowledge to come up with a business plan.

Much of her workday is spent at a computer, working on graphics, designing new websites, and maintaining established sites. She spends a good deal of time soliciting new business—making phone calls, handling advertising, and talking to prospective clients. She generally works about five hours a day, sometimes on weekends.

Susan enjoys the creativity of designing new websites and working with graphic design, although she describes maintaining the older sites as boring. She loves the creative aspect of her work and the fact that she can set her own hours. Many days, she spends the morning making phone calls and the afternoon at the beach or doing whatever else she wants to do. She often works on design and graphics projects in the evening or late at night.

Most of Susan's business has been through word of mouth, because she doesn't enjoy trying to sell her services and doesn't feel that sales is her strong suit. She says that she sometimes misses the camaraderie of working in an office, although she can get a lot done in a short period of time working alone.

Susan has some advice for others considering starting their own businesses. "I'd probably tell others to get some experience with a big company before they even consider going out on their own," she says. "Then make a business plan and try to follow it. Work out every aspect of the business in the business plan so you have a really good reason for working alone at home!"

Corina Brown, Graphic Designer

Corina Brown received her degree in graphic design and advertising from Western Washington University, where she also trained in broadcast design. After working for the Fox affiliate in Seattle for several years, she decided to strike out on her own.

Corina has always enjoyed art and found that it came easily to her. Once in college, she knew that she wanted to work in broadcast design and films. Today she is the owner and president of Corina Art and Interplanetary Design (www.corinaart.com) in Los Angeles. Corina Art features portrait art, figurative, and action pieces. Subjects include celebrities, athletes, musicians, and private collectors. Interplanetary Design is the graphic design aspect of the business, handling corporate work, merchandising, advertising, and print work.

Even though her business is established, Corina says that there is always more work to be done to keep projects coming in. She works on the Internet and through e-mail, looking for new business, making cold calls, and communicating with existing customers. She does print work from her home, but when she gets a broadcast job, she travels to the station's location to work.

Corina is very happy with her work and the success she has found in her career. She is able to tailor her job to suit her needs.

She loves being her own boss and having the opportunity to travel. What she likes least is the stress involved in finding new work. And although the work pays well and the company is successful, there are more bills to pay when running your own company.

Here is Corina's advice to others interested in a similar career: "I would advise others to figure out the direction in graphic design that seems right for them. Then I would encourage them to take a chance. Just remember that you will have to work hard to get where you want to be."

Amanda Danforth, Transcription Service

Amanda Danforth owns TypedWrite, a transcription and desktop publishing business that she runs from her home in Rhode Island. She attended the University of Rhode Island, where she earned a bachelor of science degree with a double major in education and French. Her business is a good example of one of the greatest perks of working from home: a native of Rhode Island, she began her business there, then moved to New York for several years, and has now returned to her hometown, taking TypedWrite with her each time, without any interruptions in business.

Prior to starting her own company, Amanda worked as an office manager, running three businesses from one office. This was before computers were in regular use, and the job taught her a lot about organizing her time and priorities. When someone she knew needed help at an advertising firm, she decided to take the job, which led to side projects that she was able to do on her own time.

Always observant, Amanda read newsletters, books, and bulletins with a natural eye for proofreading, finding typos that she knew she wouldn't have let get into print. She began by publishing newsletters and brochures for some big companies. Eventually, however, transcription assignments grew to fill about 80 percent of her time, putting her eye for detail to good use.

What Amanda enjoys most about working at home is the flexibility of her schedule and the ability to stay at home to raise her two sons. She can make the time to coach baseball teams, attend school events, and help out in the boys' classrooms. If something comes up at school, she can alter her work schedule to fit it in.

Amanda says that she doesn't have a typical day, because her schedule depends on her current project. If she is working on a big assignment that will take a couple of weeks, she takes care of herself before hitting the desk. Once the boys are on the school bus, she takes time for a workout before starting her project. "You have to take care of yourself when you work for yourself and by yourself!" she says. "No one else is going to do that for you!"

When asked what she likes least, she admits that sometimes it's difficult to stay focused on work, making for a less productive day and a busier schedule the next day. Being self-employed, there are times when there isn't any work, which means no money is coming in.

Amanda admits that it's very easy to be distracted by household chores or even by the ability to take breaks whenever she wants to. She's found that sticking to designated work times and taking breaks to do the housework and plan dinner works best for her. That way she can stay focused on what she's working on and still manage to get personal things taken care of.

Based on her experience, Amanda's primary advice is to stay focused. She suggests writing a business plan and sticking to it, revisiting it often and revising your plan and goals if necessary. She also believes that networking is a great tool for home-based workers and suggests joining groups and organizations that support home-based businesses.

In your own community, the chamber of commerce may have a home-based business organization. Associations such as the Rotary Club or Women in Business groups also offer networking opportunities that will let you share ideas and interact with others in your position, as well as learn about new business opportunities. "Surround yourself with successful people," Amanda advises. "You will be successful, too."

Mechelle Gooch, Office Support Services

After working as an executive assistant, Mechelle Gooch started Cooper Business Services, an office support team, out of her home in California. She started with a computer, a printer, and an additional phone line. She advertised through flyers to businesses and the newspaper and by word of mouth.

Mechelle worked for fourteen years as executive assistant to the presidents of small businesses. From these experiences, she learned how to run a small business, how to network, and how consultants are chosen for assignments.

Because she is very well organized, she was able to learn the mechanics of the job quickly, such as typing and basic office procedures. Since starting the business, Mechelle has added project management, human resources, and board-of-directors liaison to her list of services.

Mechelle says that as a business owner and mother of four, her typical days are rather hectic. She conducts business when her toddler is asleep and handles most of her client work later in the day. She enjoys the flexibility of her work, but she wishes that she had more time to build the business because she has many ideas but not the time to implement them.

For Mechelle, one of the best perks about working at home is the ability to be fully involved with her children. For example, she can provide regular weekly transportation for her daughter's softball team, something she would probably be unable to do if she worked outside the home. The only downside is that sometimes she finds it difficult to concentrate with her family around.

Mechelle offers some insight to others who hope to operate a home business. "My advice to others would be to make sure you like what you do, have a plan, and believe in yourself," she says. "My one comment to someone considering a home-based business is that you must stay focused. There are a multitude of things you will catch yourself doing instead of working if you're not careful."

Sharon Lawlor, Travel Agent and Independent Representative

Sharon Lawlor is an independent representative, travel agent, and regional manager for TravelMax International. She studied human relations and organizational behavior at the University of San Francisco, almost completing a bachelor's degree.

Sharon quit a lucrative position in insurance sales in 1996 when her son was born. When he was three months old, a company offered to set her up to work from home, which she has been doing ever since. She sells travel packages and offers tutorials that teach others to become home-based travel agents. Because Sharon loves to travel, the benefits of traveling as a professional in the industry were very appealing. In addition, selling the tutorial products had the potential to generate considerable income.

From her experience in selling insurance, Sharon knew that she enjoyed traveling and meeting new people. She wanted a new career that would allow her to travel and also provide residual income—income that she continues to receive after making an initial sale. She saw the potential for both of these options in TravelMax.

Sharon's workdays vary tremendously. Some days are quite hectic, but she can generally control the schedule and even enjoys the busy pace. Sharon works between thirty and thirty-five hours a week, whether in her home office or on travel assignments.

When asked to describe a typical day, Sharon provided this summary: She prepares breakfast for her family, checks with the company for the day's updates, and gets her son ready for his homeschool lessons. She then makes calls to her team partners in California and Pennsylvania and answers calls from people requesting information on becoming home-based travel agents. Later in the day Sharon visits the TravelMax office to turn in paperwork from a meeting she hosted the previous weekend. During the afternoon she speaks on the phone with an agent who is coordinating a trip to Hawaii and answers e-mail messages.

What she enjoys most about the work is getting to meet people across the country who enjoy traveling as much as she does. Some meetings are by telephone or e-mail, but she often does get to meet other agents and clients in person at company-sponsored regional or national meetings.

Sharon has some practical advice for anyone interested in a similar career. "Understand that any home-based business will require some expense to get it moving," she says. "While it only costs a person about $500 to become an agent with TravelMax, they will also need to purchase business cards, do advertising, and so forth. Also, plan to invest at least a year to really get your business moving. Too many people quit after the first couple of months, and that isn't enough time to judge the success or failure of any business. The only way to succeed in any business is to make the commitment to work on it at least an hour a day.

"I would advise people not to listen to anyone who tells them they can get rich quick or any other such claim. What works for one person won't work for everyone. To be successful in this business, you have to want and like to travel, have a desire to build your future, and be willing to talk to people and help them to succeed!"

Debi Devitt, Secretarial Service

Debi Devitt runs Devitt's Secretarial Service out of her home in California. She went to a community college, gained some office experience, and then took a word-processing course prior to starting her own business.

Like other home business owners, Debi started her company in order to be at home with her child. She had previously tried child care and delivering newspapers but wasn't happy with either of these options. Because she had enjoyed working in an office and liked secretarial work, her father-in-law suggested that she start a home secretarial service. She began her business in 1990.

After taking her children to school, Debi checks e-mail messages and starts to work. She usually works until 2 P.M., taking breaks to do household chores throughout the day. After bringing her children home from school and helping them with their homework, she works for another hour or so in the afternoon. Depending on her workload, she either takes the evening off or works again, sometimes until 10 P.M.

Debi loves her job for the variety it offers. She may have a few letters to type or a tape to transcribe, but the phone can ring at any time and bring a new assignment. The number of hours she works per week varies, but is usually between twenty and thirty. Tight deadlines can be stressful, but projects without deadlines are easier to manage.

The top priority for Debi, however, is the ability to be available to her children. Bringing them to school and home again are an established part of her routine. In addition, if they have a day off or are sick, she doesn't have to arrange for child care.

What Debi likes least about her work is the isolation. "Sometimes I want to talk to someone besides my dog!" she says. "Another downside is the instability of work flow. It's hard to get a steady stream; it's either way too busy or too slow.

"In addition, some clients think that because you work at home they can call you at nine at night to discuss work. Quite frankly, I'm in no mood to conduct business after 6 P.M.—even if I'm working.

"Also, sometimes family and friends think that because you work at home, you can watch their kids for them all the time or run errands for them. Ha! I barely get my own errands done."

Debi's advice to anyone considering a career similar to hers is to have a lot of patience. Building a clientele takes time, and you need to be patient and persistent while you establish your company. She also says, "Every day, do something to market your business, and eventually it will pay off."

Karen Martin, Health Business Consultant

Karen Martin earned her bachelor of science degree in microbiology from Pennsylvania State University in 1980 and her master of arts in education from California State University, Bakersfield, in 1985. Today, she serves as president of her own health consulting business based out of her home in Santa Monica, California.

Although Karen had considered starting her own business, she decided to stay in her job in the corporate world and save money to buy a house. When she was offered a promotion to vice president, Karen realized that she didn't want the additional pressure of the new position, which would be politically difficult and demanding. In addition, she thought that the offered compensation package was not sufficient. After weighing the options, she resigned from the company in 1993 and started her own consulting business. She says, "It was the most empowering and career-defining decision I've made!"

Karen has worked in health care for her entire career. She originally considered studying medicine but decided on a less arduous path. She is a licensed medical technologist and now spends her days on the business aspects of health care rather than working in a clinical environment. In retrospect, she believes that every position she's held has provided a natural progression to the next.

Karen's days vary quite a bit. During quiet periods, she starts to work by 9 A.M. On Monday, Wednesday, and Friday, she works until 3:30 so that she can attend an afternoon yoga class. When she is busier, Karen sometimes works ten-hour days.

The projects also vary. Karen's clients are HMOs, physician groups, therapists, and hospitals. She conducts meetings outside of her home office but does most of the actual work at home. She tries to limit travel to the East Coast and Midwest to only two or three projects a year. Each project generally lasts several months, and Karen usually handles only two projects at a time. She sometimes hires outside help but generally does all of the work herself.

For Karen, running a home-based business allows her the ability to make choices. She says, "The upside of all of this is the freedom—freedom to choose the projects I like, work with people I like; freedom to work at 5 A.M. if I choose or take off two hours during the day for a long lunch with a friend. Also, I don't mind working alone—that's a big hurdle for many home-based people to get over. Some people find the isolation intolerable. I quite like it. Plus, I meet with clients and colleagues frequently enough that I don't stagnate in my home."

When asked about the downside, Karen mentions not having administrative and technical support. Although she doesn't need administrative assistance on a regular basis, when she does need it it's difficult to do without. For example, if she has to spend time dealing with a computer crash, it can throw off her schedule and make it difficult to meet deadlines.

Another downside is not having a regular income. "But I've become very comfortable with the not-knowing aspect of self-employment," she says. "I have complete trust that the money will come in when it needs to, and for seven years, I've been okay."

For anyone interested in starting a consulting career, Karen recommends being sure that you have a marketable service or product or developing a skill that will make you a hot commodity. The ability to provide service to your clients in a way that most large organizations can't is an important aspect of successful self-employment.

Karen advises having a minimum of six months' savings to fall back on before you give up a steady job. She also stresses the importance of being sure that you can work alone for long periods of time, and of having the self-discipline to stick to your schedule and get the work done. Like many others who work at home, Karen also recommends that you make sure friends and family realize that you are really working, not sitting at home waiting for visitors.

Ramond Silverstein, Small Business Advisory Board

Ramond Silverstein took his broad business experience, skills, and affinity for helping others and founded a unique home-based business in 1993. Aware that many entrepreneurs often have to work within a vacuum, making decisions on their own without the advantage of other viewpoints, he created PRO: President's Resource Organization. PRO is an advisory board that provides small-business owners with the outsider's view they lack. The group can act as a sounding board or even as a board of directors for a company and infuse the business with new ideas.

Ray explains that, with advisory boards, company owners can draw on the expertise of people in a variety of fields who may have often dealt with the same issues the business owner is now confronting for the first time. The board can offer a variety of approaches or solutions that have worked for them.

The best advisory boards are made up of people from a mix of backgrounds, who bring to the table a wide range of experiences and expertise. The mix also ensures that no matter what issue is brought up, there's probably at least one board member who has some knowledge or insights to offer.

As corporate downsizing continues, an increasing number of people are launching their own businesses. While they may have expertise in the fields they choose, as their businesses grow, they run into issues they may have never dealt with as an employee. From handling personnel problems to developing a marketing plan, these owners probably have few others with whom to discuss sensitive matters.

In addition to offering input, advisory boards can spur business owners into action. While the board won't have any control over what owners ultimately do, they will expect to hear about the progress made. This makes the owners accountable to someone other than themselves and can keep them from putting things off.

Advisory boards can also make a business owner's life simpler. The problem that seems so insurmountable when the owner looks at it on his or her own may be quite routine to one of the board members.

Ray reports that his home-based business allows him a relaxed schedule, an informal atmosphere, and the ability to work within his own time frames. "The number of hours per week that I put in is my decision," he says.

"The best part of this career is meeting interesting people," offers Ray. "It also allows me to be reactive and to serve as a problem solver. And in offering some options for business owners, I feel that I am providing help to others."

Dr. Elliot McGucken, Web Entrepreneur

Dr. Elliot McGucken earned his bachelor of arts degree in physics from Princeton University and his doctorate from the University of North Carolina at Chapel Hill. Today he serves as president of Classicals and jollyroger.com LLC based in Davidson, North Carolina. He also teaches physics and programming at the University of North Carolina at Chapel Hill and has published a book of poetry, a novel, and a collection of essays, in addition to several scientific papers.

Classicals and jollyroger.com, described on its website as "the world's classical portal," is a comprehensive site where visitors can share a love of literary classics. Elliott attributes his success with jollyroger.com to his early love of reading and his strong science and math abilities. His training in physics in both college and graduate school gave him a solid technical background and taught him to find answers to questions about how things work. Elliott says, "This attitude helps with the constantly developing frontier of the World Wide Web, where one day webmasters must optimize a Perl security script, and the next day they have to configure an Apache Web server to allow poetry to be posted by registered visitors."

The idea for the jollyroger.com project came to Elliott when he was a graduate student. Working at a UNIX workstation in the early days of the Internet, he posted some of his poetry in HTML on a Web page. Today the site serves more than one hundred thousand page views a day to more than two hundred thousand unique monthly visitors.

Elliott has been fascinated by the Internet since it began. He says, "The Internet was and is so perfectly free and thus exciting. I remember I posted my poems one day, and the next day some girl from Ireland wrote me about how cool she thought they were. I guess that's when the size and the scope of the Internet hit home with me."

Elliott describes running an online start-up business as "a wild ride, the decathlon of jobs." He appreciates the freedom and the potential for growth that the Internet offers as a publishing medium. For example, while jollyroger.com started as a literary magazine, it has grown into a context-centered portal about great books.

Running jollyroger.com has given Elliott the opportunity to make his passion his profession, and he enjoys the daily responsibilities that come with the job. On any workday, he is usually involved with a combination of activities, including working on a collection of poetry and prose from the website, writing and editing original works for the site, answering fan e-mail, scanning photos and editing graphical content for the site, configuring servers and working with software, and updating affiliate relationships with companies such as Amazon.com and Dell.

Elliott enjoys the variety of challenges that mastering the Web provides. He says that he is never bored with his work, and his passion is fueled by his belief in jollyroger.com as a means of bringing the classics to life for thousands of users. On the downside, Elliott says, "My least favorite thing is backing everything up and then making backups of the backups, but it must be done, for jollyroger.com is nothing but data on a disk."

When asked what advice he would give to anyone considering running a Web-based business, Elliott addresses the personal gratification that can come from following a dream. "I would tell others who are considering this type of work—follow your passions!"

he enthuses. "Whenever you are visited by a powerful passion, cherish it and harness it, for passion is the seed of all that is worthwhile in this world. If you follow your passions, money might not come in the beginning, but eventually wealth that cannot be counted in dollars from the mint shall be created. This is perhaps a lesson attested to by every author who has ever written an enduring literary work. Many of the brave and original souls died penniless, but what they created was priceless—our very heritage and all the underlying foundations of our language, laws, and civilization.

"And that's one of the greatest things about this country and about the Internet—they allow and encourage us to follow our passions, and they often reward us for doing so."

Rosa Pearl, Psychic

Rosa Pearl is based in Englewood, Ohio, where she serves as the home-based director of Doorway to Universal Healing. Her career began in 1991 when she joined a psychic fair circuit, developed a clientele, and made appointments to do readings and esoteric work from her home.

After the births of her last two children, Rosa wanted to be a stay-at-home parent. She realized that she had a gift of intuition and decided to explore it. She became classified as a clairvoyant, clairaudient, clairsentient, and psychometric and began to do reading as her main occupation.

Many of Rosa's clients were interested in dream interpretation, which gave her the opportunity to practice her skill and to teach it to others. Sometimes clients would invite up to ten guests to their homes, where Rosa would teach in the evenings or on weekends. This grew into invitations from metaphysical bookstores to speak and teach about dreams. She also received similar requests from spiritual retreats.

Rosa's experiences as a natural clairvoyant and clairaudient began in childhood and intensified as she grew older. She worked in management positions, where she learned the skills needed to delegate, arbitrate, and supervise a group. Although she was initially overwhelmed by the offer to serve as director of the Doorway to Universal Healing, Rosa's ambition to work at home remained her main priority. By combining her natural skills with those she had acquired in previous jobs, she was able to develop a plan that allowed her to pursue her new career. "Consistency was the key," she says. "Make the goal and stick to it. Improvise—and stay on track. The challenge of being a psychic is the insight that I can offer my clients to help them make the most of the choices they have concerning career and life."

Rosa became interested in shamanism, and during her apprenticeship she learned that the altered state of consciousness for a shamanic journey was easy to achieve. She explains that while shamans are known for working in esoteric realms, Reiki masters have a reputation for being hands on. By combining these two methods, she works in the aura of the client. Rosa is also an independent contractor for PsychicChat.net, where she does random and scheduled online readings that pertain to the Doorway to Universal Healing.

A typical day starts at 8:45 A.M., when Rosa logs on to the Web to check her appointments for online readings and teachings. At 11:45 A.M., lunch includes a trip to the post office and other errands. Between 1 and 3 P.M., she holds shamanic appointments. At 2:30, the children start returning home from school, and homework and chores begin after her last shamanic appointment. She says that evenings are difficult, because she has scheduled readings three nights a week from 5 P.M. to 8 P.M. or 9: P.M. to midnight. Her paid working hours total about twenty-five to thirty-five a week.

Rosa enjoys meeting the variety of people she encounters through her work and says that she is busy and relaxed most of the time. She describes her working atmosphere as quiet, pleasant, and soothing. "That is one of the perks of having a home office. Your work environment is what you make it. To display the art decor of my choice, I chose cream walls accented by hanging plants, vines that crawl, and potted trees, along with a fountain that trickles."

Rosa also derives great satisfaction from her clients' positive reactions to her readings. Whether she interprets a dream or helps a CEO to focus on different aspects of her business, hearing feedback about how her work helped another is very gratifying. It is also exciting when a skeptic comes for an initial reading expecting to find that psychic abilities are fake but leaves believing what Rosa has told her.

Rosa points out that the financial reality of working as a psychic can be difficult. Income develops slowly, and you must be a good salesperson to maximize your income potential. Unfortunately some clients think that because psychic ability is a gift, readings should be free. As nice as this might sound, for anyone trying to earn a living, it is not a possibility.

When asked how she would advise someone interested in working as a psychic, Rosa stresses the importance of keeping your current job until you begin to get established in your new career. Her suggestions are specific: "Build your clientele first. Let your clientele grow until it infringes on your day job, then give your two weeks' notice and get your office and reading room in order. Make sure you have two overstuffed chairs for yourself and your client. This puts you both at ease. Get an egg timer and set it for your allotted time. I allow my clients to purchase fifteen minutes or thirty minutes. When the bell rings, wish them well and walk them to the door. Some clients will infringe on your personal time. Become hard-nosed about this issue. Learn the difference between the words *need* and *want*. The client who always states, 'I need,' usually only wants your undivided attention. You may have to create an eight-by-ten-inch sign that cleverly addresses the issues of need and want.

"In closing, I would say—may your career choice be blessed in all ways, always!"

Maria Holtz, Bookkeeper

Maria Holtz works as a supervising senior bookminder at Book-minders (www.bookminders.com) in Pittsburgh, Pennsylvania. This unique company relies on an entirely home-based workforce that provides outsourced bookkeeping services to 150 companies and nonprofits. The firm has drawn national attention as a model for telecommuting success. All of Bookminders's forty employees work from home and telecommute via fax and e-mail.

The company has put into place several guidelines to ensure that workers are productive—each employee must have a home office with a door, pay is based on work completed, and so forth—while also allowing them the freedom to work, for the most part, when they want to. The originator of this unique business model, Tom Joseph, Bookminders's founder and president, has been featured in the *Wall Street Journal* and *Entrepreneur Magazine*'s "Business Start-Ups."

Maria earned her bachelor's degree from West Virginia University, followed by a master's in public accounting and her C.P.A. certification. She started working for Bookminders in 1996, after the company was recommended by a partner in a C.P.A. firm that had done some work for her previous company.

Maria was mainly attracted by the idea of working at home. As the mother of a four-year-old, she felt that she had already missed out on a lot of her son's life. She also disliked working a strict nine-to-five routine, and because most of her previous jobs had required more than a forty-hour week, Maria felt ready to slow down and revise her schedule. She liked the idea of being in control of her work environment and hours—she prefers not to work in the early morning and likes to work at night after her children are in bed. Working for Bookminders makes this schedule possible.

One of the things that Maria disliked about her earlier jobs was dealing with office politics and difficult people. She says, "I encountered many individuals who were willing to step on anyone to get ahead, and I found that I did not handle these situations well. I took an assertiveness training course, and that helped."

Most of Maria's colleagues at Bookminders share her desire for a balance of home and work life. Although the staff generally works autonomously, they do function well as a team. Maria credits the company's structure and goals with making this possible and finds it a refreshing change from other jobs she has held.

When asked to describe her schedule, Maria talks about her responsibilities during a typical week at Bookminders. She has nine clients, and her work begins with setting up new accounts. In this capacity, she establishes a new client's initial financial information in the company's system and works on developing a customized program to meet the client's needs. In addition to her regular duties, Maria has other administrative responsibilities since she is a supervising senior bookminder.

Maria visits each client's office once a week. She tries to schedule all of her appointments on Mondays and Wednesdays, which reduces the need for child care on those days. On Monday mornings she takes her son to school and her daughter to the babysitter and heads to her client meetings. Most of the office visits last from fifteen minutes to an hour. She drops off the financial information that she's processed in the previous week, reviews new information for the current week's work, and discusses any questions or problems with the client. She is usually finished with client visits in time to pick up her children at three and spends the afternoon helping her son with his homework and playing with her daughter. Monday evenings are hectic family time, so Maria usually doesn't do much more than check and answer e-mail messages.

Tuesday, Wednesday, and Thursday are generally flexible days in Maria's schedule. She does client work or other administrative work. She is also able to run errands, do housework, or take care of other personal matters during this time, when stores are generally less crowded than in the evenings or on weekends. Maria usually knows how much work she needs to do and how long it will take and tries to schedule her work time around whatever else she has planned for that week. If she has a busy weekend scheduled and has a lot of work to complete, she'll sometimes ask the babysitter to work an extra day so that she has more uninterrupted time to complete her own work. Maria likes to spend evenings and weekends with her family, so she tries not to work at those times. If she must work, however, her husband will take care of the children while she attends to her business.

Maria visits two clients on Wednesday afternoons and attends administrative meetings on Friday. Most of the Bookminders staff members are required to attend one monthly staff meeting. She occasionally assists in leading the meetings or meets with other bookminders to review accounts and discuss design and quality assurance issues. To keep up with her schedule, she generally has meetings every Friday.

Periodically Maria assists in training a new staff member or will transition one of her clients to a new bookminder. In these cases, she coordinates her schedule with that of the other bookminder and the client, which usually involves one client visit. On the other hand, training a new employee involves several hours working together at the employee's home.

Maria most enjoys the flexibility and work environment that her job allows. She credits telecommunications, advanced technology, and the company's support with making this possible. Maria praises Bookminders for its position as a family-oriented company. She explains that during her first pregnancy, she worked at a job with very long hours and a high level of stress, which she believes contributed to a difficult pregnancy and complicated birth. Her son was in full-time day care until he was four, and in those early years he was often sick and required tubes in his ears due to frequent ear infections. Maria says, "I blame a lot of this on myself and my attempts at juggling a stressful job and the care of a child. With my second pregnancy, I was able to take good care of myself (and nap in the afternoons if I wanted to). The pregnancy and birth went much smoother, and my daughter is a very happy, healthy child. (My son is happy and healthy now, too, but I wish I'd been able to give him a better start.)"

Although she fully enjoys working at home, Maria acknowledges that it's not always as easy as you might think. It requires a lot of commitment and self-motivation, as well as a supportive family and flexible child care arrangements. For example, she had difficulty finding child care for six months after her daughter was born, and this made her job much more difficult. There are also times when she simply has more work than usual and needs to work on weekends, or one of her children is sick. These times can be difficult on both Maria and her family, and this is what she likes the least about working at home.

"To others I'd recommend that you take your job seriously," Maria advises. "Working at home is a real job, despite what some people may think. You can get out of the job exactly what you put into it. But, if you really make it work for you, you will get much more in all aspects of your life."

Service Careers at Home

In this chapter, we met Susan Sheehan, a website consultant; Amanda Danforth, who runs a transcription service; Mechelle Gooch, who heads an office support team; Sharon Lawlor, a travel agent and independent representative; Debi Devitt, who offers a secretarial service; Karen Martin, a health business consultant; Ramond Silverstein, who heads a consulting advisory board firm; Dr. Elliot McGucken, a Web entrepreneur; Rosa Pearl, a psychic; and Maria Holtz, a bookkeeper.

Needless to say, these individuals offer a large cross section of career areas and have widely differing backgrounds and experiences. However, they all decided to take a chance on something they deeply believed in. With a great deal of hard work and perseverance, they are all trying to make their offerings successful.

In my own experience as a full-time freelance writer for the past fifteen years—and therefore a home-based small-business owner offering a service—I personally know what it is like to wear the many hats of the self-employed. It is a challenge, to say the least. You must always be aware of all of the facets of your business—marketing, completing assignments, staying close to impending projects, taking care of billing, keeping up with correspondence, approaching new markets, networking, staying current in your profession, attending conferences, and so forth. There is a great deal of juggling that accompanies anyone who is successful in this kind of career. But I wouldn't have it any other way. To me, it is the fulfillment of a childhood dream.

CHAPTER SEVEN

Human Resources Homebodies

There is no substitute for hard work.
—Thomas A. Edison

uman resources professionals are involved in helping people find appropriate employment and making sure that individuals are placed in the best possible positions at various companies. In these capacities, they perform a very important service.

Human Resources Professionals

Because so many human resources professionals are able to work at home, an entire chapter has been devoted to them. As you read, you will discover some common themes as well as a wide range of situations, one of which might be of special interest to you.

Laura J. Stoll, Corporate Entertainment

Laura J. Stoll is the founder and business director of The Riot Act, a Chicago-based company that offers services designed to make corporate meetings more effective, engaging, and fun. She studied at Marist College in Poughkeepsie, New York, where she earned a bachelor of science in business administration with a concentration in information systems.

Laura worked for eight years as a management consultant with KPMG (now BearingPoint Consulting), focusing primarily on banking systems strategies and operations. As her career progressed, she worked more closely with bank management reporting requirements relative to international capital standards, work that involved 100 percent travel to client sites across the United States and Europe.

The idea for The Riot Act (www.the-riot-act.com) came to Laura through her husband's work as an improvisational actor. As she learned about the corporate entertainment world, she saw more and more ways to improve it—but didn't feel quite ready for the challenges and uncertainty of self-employment.

When she left KPMG, Laura took a job with a new company that ultimately gave her the final push to start her own business. She found herself working in a negative environment where change was unwelcome and the management style was oppressive. She resigned from this position after only eight months, promising herself that she would never again allow herself to work in such a negative atmosphere. As unpleasant as the experience was, however, it gave her the impetus to take the first step toward self-employment. She wrote a business plan and decided to take a chance on her ideas.

The services offered by The Riot Act vary depending on clients' needs. The company's services, which Laura calls "Meeting Content Solutions," include incorporating improvisational acting performances, facilitated discussions, team-building exercises, and training into uniquely interactive sessions. The company employs professional actors who travel to client locations, using their creative talents to energize employees and improve performance and productivity. For example, a meeting entertainment service is intended to energize the audience by using humor and audience participation. A program might include a quiz show based on the client's products, a talk show featuring management staff, or an improvised segment based on audience suggestions. Team-building activities might include themed scavenger hunts or physical team exercises. The Riot Act also works with a professional trainer who helps clients enhance their presentation skills.

Although fairly new, The Riot Act is already showing signs of success. The company's first performance was for the president and CFO of a globally recognized company, who loved the innovative solutions offered. Laura says, "The personal sign of success for me was the reactions—of the audience, of the client, and of the team. Hearing veteran performers say that this was the most positive corporate experience of their career was a dream."

When asked what she likes most about having a home-based business, Laura's first reaction is "No more commute!" which is followed closely by not having to wear uncomfortable shoes and no office politics. Working from home allows her to spend more time with her husband. She enjoys having the autonomy to set her own priorities, dealing with whatever is most important at the time, even if that means taking care of personal matters in the middle of the day.

In addition, Laura likes having the flexibility to work wherever she feels comfortable, whether in her office or at a coffee shop. Being self-employed has freed her from feeling chained to a desk. The only negative that she finds is not being covered under a group health insurance plan, which is a major issue for so many home-based business owners.

Laura's responsibilities as business director are varied. She handles client contact, finding new business for the company, and takes care of all financial matters. She also spends a lot of time working on project plans, making sure all aspects of the events are in place and running smoothly. Finding material for performances is also part of her job—Laura recently spent a day researching a British football song for an upcoming karaoke event for a global client.

Given all these duties, it's apparent that Laura doesn't have a typical workday—which is fine with her. She tries to work when she needs to, whether that means waking at 6 A.M. to start work by 7 A.M., or running errands in the morning and then working until midnight. She's found that what's best for her is to manage work tasks right alongside her other everyday chores, identifying priorities a day in advance to be sure she knows what needs to be done.

"I finally feel like I have found the right balance between my work life and my personal life," she says. "Work doesn't happen between nine and five; office hours do. And since I no longer work in an office, my work can happen whenever it is best for me to do it."

In general, however, Laura's daily schedule is to wake and dress at 7 A.M. and have breakfast while surfing the Internet, checking personal mail, and reading the daily news. Next she'll work on whatever the day's big project is, which involves sitting at her desk, listening to headphones, and using the computer. She usually breaks for lunch at 1 or 2 P.M. and likes to spend the afternoon on something unrelated to work, like running errands, doing housework, or managing personal matters. About 50 percent of the time, she'll return to her desk and work several more hours in the evening.

Laura has some good advice for other potential home workers. "Make your work space comfortable," she suggests. "Indulge yourself in the little things that would not fly in the corporate setting. (I used to freeze in corporate offices, and always joked about wanting to have a blanket at my chair. You can bet I have that blanket now!)

"Make a habit out of scheduling appointments outside of the home. At the very least, even in the coldest of winter months, getting out even just once a week is important."

Susan Zitron, Career Coach and Team Builder

Susan Zitron attended Ohio State University and presently works as a career coach and team builder in California. She is a partner

in Zitron Pharma Career Services (www.zitroncareerservices
.com) in San Francisco. She is the author of *Coaching for the Life
of Your Career*, a handbook/workbook that she self-publishes and
sells.

Susan attended many personal effectiveness workshops in the
1980s. She also took a course in neurolinguistic programming and
believes that this, combined with a strong spiritual path in meta-
physics, has strengthened her effectiveness as a coach.

Most of Susan's education as a career coach and team builder
was gained from on-the-job experience. Prior to career coaching,
she spent twenty years working in sales of broadcast media,
telecommunications equipment, and long distance services,
plus more than ten years of personnel placement and executive
recruitment.

In the seventies, Susan was employed as a placement counselor,
working in both temporary and permanent positions. In the
eighties she worked as an executive recruiter, and in the nineties
she was an outplacement counselor. It was while working in this
last position that she realized how few people knew how to effectively market themselves. The nineties saw a great deal of layoffs
and downsizing, leaving many people in need of career coaching.

Susan feels that she is very effective in helping people to achieve
their career goals, based on a model she created called a Personal
Career Business Plan. This copyrighted model helps people to
understand and maximize their personal success factors. Combined with her ability to coach people in everything they must say,
do, or write to be considered a top candidate, the model has
helped her and her clients to achieve success.

In 1991 Susan joined an outplacement firm dedicated to helping professionals find employment by using the same marketing
principles that most companies use to market and sell products.
The next year she started her own company, Zitron Career Services, based on the needs and concerns of a focus group of six
senior managers she had helped return to the job market.

Since forming the company, Susan has worked successfully with many companies, providing team-building exercises and reemployment or outplacement services. She has also had success as an executive coach, helping many professionals to advance in their careers. In addition, Susan coaches people back into the job market after a period of unemployment. She has received coaching requests from people around the world.

Susan believes that people should use all of their skills to achieve something bigger than anything they have done before. In her own case, that includes her sales and marketing background and the work she has done as a recruiter and outplacement counselor. Combined with her spiritual belief that people are inherently successful and deserving of satisfying work, this makes her daily goal one of helping people to uncover and maximize their personal success style.

Susan's job primarily involves talking with people, either in her office or by telephone. On days when she has to work with clients on the East Coast, she starts work at 7 A.M. and might work until 8 P.M. Usually, however, she works from 9:30 to 6:30. Susan generally works five and a half days a week, scheduling Saturday morning meetings for clients who have jobs.

The goal of Susan's work is to uncover people's beliefs and career values and to identify what has made them successful so far. She feels that she is protecting her clients' best interests to help correct any existing problems and avoid creating new ones.

Susan finds the atmosphere of her home office very relaxing. She works in a comfortable and spacious room with a fireplace, patio, and view of the hills. She often listens to classical music while she works and occasionally enjoys the serenity of a fire.

Susan loves her work because she believes it is what she does best. Most of her clients successfully achieve their goals, and she receives many letters of thanks that provide fulfillment. She enjoys the freedom to create a coaching plan as she and the client progress, which she wasn't able to do in the corporate world. She also appreciates being able to take time off when she wants to or to work any hours she chooses. For instance, Susan wrote her book in three weeks straight, working around the clock.

The only downside has been when the client roster is inconsistent and several months have gone by without income. Otherwise, she thoroughly enjoys her job.

Susan offers some carefully considered advice to others considering her career field. She says, "Be totally committed to having great results, even when the client cannot see it. It's important to prepare yourself financially as best you can, keep your overhead low, network in associations where people who would hire you participate, and then volunteer in those associations as often as possible so they can see who you are and get to know you. I am very well known in my association and value it greatly.

"Once you feel secure, step out of your safety zone and do things you have never done before—present a workshop, be a guest speaker, write an article, author a book, be a community leader.

"Find a spiritual or religious path from which you find a great reservoir of inspiration, uplifting feelings, validation, support, love, and forgiveness. You cannot give it to others if you don't have it within yourself first. Don't waste time being unhappy.

"Expect that things will change, even the best-laid plans, and use it as an opportunity to challenge your thinking. And trust that there is always a solution to everything."

Kathleen M. Richter, Human Resources Consultant

Kathleen Richter earned her bachelor of arts degree in sociology from the University of Missouri and her master of science degree in human resources management from Houston Baptist University. She entered the world of human resources management upon her college graduation in 1977 by working in the student placement office. After twenty years of experience in that field, she currently serves as a human resources consultant in San Francisco, California.

Kathleen was initially attracted to her field by the variety of skills and knowledge required to master the human resources profession—staffing, employee benefits, employee compensation, safety, legal compliance, policy development, project implementation, budgeting, and training. She saw this as a potential lifelong career, one with which she wouldn't become bored.

Workdays can vary greatly. Some days Kathleen spends entirely in her home office. Other times she makes daily visits to a client site. Still other days are a combination of the two. Clients range from a fifty-employee start-up to a Fortune 500 company that employs twenty thousand. Depending on the workload, she might be working with only one client, or she might handle several simultaneously.

The number of hours Kathleen works depends on how many clients she is managing or the intensity of a single project. She has the option to decline projects, which allows her the freedom to take time off for weeks or months at a time. While some weeks she might not work at all, during others she will log more than fifty hours.

The job offers diversity because each project is as different as the client company. Some clients are very clear about the work they want done. Others have difficulty articulating their needs, so Kathleen must first perform a needs assessment. Based on the assessment, she can then make recommendations to the client and begin her work. She is never bored with her career because of the variety she encounters in every project.

Kathleen sums up by saying, "I think I'm one of the luckiest people I know. Doing this kind of work is perfect for me and brings many rewards. But I was willing to take the risk of self-employment and work hard to make it happen.

"I would recommend that others who are considering self-employment learn everything they can about their profession. Meet everyone you can meet and stay abreast of changes to your profession."

Dan Eastman, Human Resources Recruiter

Dan Eastman earned a bachelor of science degree in business administration from the University of Utah in Salt Lake City, majoring in marketing. Working college summers in an oil refinery as a tradesperson helper, he learned about pipe fitters, machinists, tool and dye makers, welders, electricians, and so forth. This later helped him to recruit people with these skills in his first recruiting assignment. Dan spent thirty years in corporate human resources management, both international and domestic, before he established Personnel Services, Inc., in 1990 to focus on placing human resources professionals in interim assignments and regular employment.

Dan had close to fifteen years of successful retail management experience working for large chains and independents, vendors and manufacturers, particularly in the garment district of New York. He worked with employees, customers, and administrative support staff, developing a good understanding of how to work well with all types of people and how to get people to work together.

Dan does most of his work from his home office, which has a private bathroom and is separate from the rest of the house. Two full-length windows overlook a landscaped area. The atmosphere is very relaxing, pleasant, and quiet.

Dan's workday begins at about 9 A.M. He reads the newspaper in depth, looking for any items that might be useful in his business. For example, company activities that may be disruptive to employees could lead to a need for recruiting services. He checks messages and e-mail and returns calls, then spends most of the rest of the day on the phone and the Internet or keeping appointments.

He describes his business as divided between two functions. One is developing or following up on leads, which involves calling potential clients who may need human resources professional staffing for an interim assignment or for a project of one type or another. The other function is filling openings that have been developed, which is essentially networking. Dan describes his business as being as much *who* you know as *what* you know, because the ideal candidate is typically not looking for a new assignment or career opportunity. While the Internet has been of great value in developing candidates, it is only really helpful in combination with personal associations.

Dan's days are busy; he generally works until 6 or 7 P.M. He seldom works on weekends and even tries to keep Friday and Monday free for four-day weekends. This was successful for a while, but business has increased substantially because more companies are finding it difficult to locate people to fill openings. When Dan schedules meetings with clients or when it is inconvenient for human resources professionals to come to his office, he makes every effort not to schedule appointments during commute hours.

Dan finds it hard to say anything negative about his career. He acknowledges that occasionally clients can be very demanding, which can be detrimental to the assignment.

Overall, Dan is pleased with his career choice and with his personal success. He says, "For someone who is accustomed to a paycheck on a regular basis, the uncertainty of income can be a major obstacle in having your own consulting practice or business such as mine. It is like any business—you need capital and staying power. If someone is income dependent, it can be a killer. As a second income, it can be great as long as you don't begin to think of it as fixed income and obligate yourself accordingly.

"For me, this career couldn't get any better. I can work as much or as little as I want. I don't have to commute. I don't have to deal with unpleasant people. My time is my own. And it's fun, interesting, and exciting!"

Ideas for Your Own Path

Laura J. Stoll, Susan Zitron, Kathleen M. Richter, and Dan Eastman—all profiled in this chapter—are dedicated human resources professionals who are effectively using a home-based setup to make the best use of their resources. If you have an inclination in this direction, perhaps they have provided some information that you can use to get started toward fulfilling your passion.

CHAPTER EIGHT

Communications Homebodies

I never did a day's work in my life. It was all fun.
—Thomas A. Edison

n today's world, the fields of advertising, public relations, and other forms of communications are enjoying a strong showing. These areas have a lot of potential for those who have strong communications skills. Are you well spoken? Can you put words together in a meaningful way? Do you enjoy the challenge of conveying information? Perhaps a career in one of these fields would be of interest to you. And you don't have to worry about trudging to the office and spending eight or ten hours a day there. Home-based professionals are successfully working in these fields in ever-increasing numbers. Here's how some of them have created communications careers at home.

Advertising, Public Relations, and Communications Professionals

The following accounts by homebodies who specialize in advertising, public relations, and communications will give you some insight into this type of work.

Karen L. Sullivan, Advertising, Public Relations, and Graphics

Karen Sullivan began her career in public relations working for a college, writing news releases for campus activities. She was given more responsibilities once her employers became aware of her design ability, and eventually she was designing brochures for the school.

A natural curiosity and inherent eye for design have served Karen well. She can critically assess an advertisement and see whether anything should have been done differently. When she worked at the college, Karen asked the artists many questions about the designs. She began to read about graphics on her own and learned that she had a natural ability in the field.

In her next position, Karen worked as manager for a Delaware printer that published a weekly advertising tabloid. Using a compugraphic typesetter, she created all the designs and hand placed the copy. She realized how much she liked working with shapes and color, which she still enjoys because of the continuous challenges that it offers.

Karen's jobs have always included other responsibilities besides design. She worked with the owner of the printing company to promote the business, learning marketing skills along the way. Whenever she was faced with a new business task, she asked questions of others in the field and read what she could about the subject.

Karen considers promotion, marketing, design, advertising, and graphics to be part of a complete package that describes the services she offers. She feels very fortunate to be able to work from her home, away from the tense atmosphere of the offices where she worked as many as fifty to sixty hours a week. Her earlier jobs were made stressful due to deadlines, equipment problems, and difficult customers. Now she can choose her customers and work when she wants to.

What Karen likes most about her work is the sense of accomplishment it gives her. She enjoys learning about different businesses and incorporating that knowledge into her designs. For Karen, the opportunity to create designs is exhilarating.

"I love working with words and presenting them to the world in an artistic and easy-to-understand format," says Karen. "The best thing is the reaction from people when they see the work. Most of the time they are in love with it and cannot believe how much it reflects what they do. Sometimes they want little changes and are afraid I will be upset. But I don't have a problem with that."

What Karen likes least about her work is the level of inconsistency in the business. "The market is competitive; the people want everything for nothing. That frustrates me," she says. "When I told a friend my rates she was shocked and said, 'Oh, well, I wouldn't pay that.' I said, 'Well, then, you will shop around and see that most agencies charge four times that much. Then you will call me.' I never apologize for my fees."

In her own business, Karen has clients sign a written proposal that clearly states her rates and asks for one-third of the money up front. At the final proof stage, she has the client review the proof and sign their approval; after this point, the client will bear the cost of any changes. Another one-third of the project cost is paid at this time. She receives the final payment after the project is printed.

Karen has some specific advice for others who are considering striking out in the design field. She stresses the importance of being aware of the market and understanding the demographics of that market; this will help you to understand how best to market a product and how to design a campaign.

She also suggests keeping good records and getting clients' signed approvals at each stage of the project. This is important to make sure there are no misunderstandings, which can be costly.

Susan Ditz, Marketing Communications Consultant and Professional Journalist

Susan Ditz is the owner of SMD Communications in Pescadero, California. She has been a marketing communications consultant and professional journalist for more than twenty-five years. After earning a bachelor of science degree in journalism from Boston University, she took a job as assistant editor of a weekly newspaper chain based in Worcester, Massachusetts.

A former *San Jose Mercury News* columnist, Susan has published work in the *San Jose Business Journal, Cruising World,* the *Stanford Lawyer, 3-2-1 Contact,* the *San Francisco Examiner,* and *Zoo Views.* She has also provided a wide range of consulting and editorial services to McDonald's, Sun Microsystems, Apple Computer, Fresh Choice Restaurants, the Palo Alto Medical Foundation, American Cancer Society, and Nabisco Confections.

Susan has always loved to read and describes herself as a "classic underachiever" who only excelled at writing. She especially enjoyed being on the staff of the school newspaper in middle school and high school and attributes at least part of this interest to the inspiration she received from a high school teacher, a former *Newsweek* writer who encouraged her to develop her skills and to consider a career in journalism.

Susan finds being a writer to be an enormously fulfilling job. She says, "One of the greatest rewards has been learning that something I wrote was the impetus for a positive change in someone's life. It also has given me an acceptable reason to satisfy my curiosity about many subjects—to ask lots and lots of questions of some fascinating people over the years—and get paid for it. It's been lots of fun to share interesting discoveries and, on occasion, I have been able to very publicly acknowledge an important contribution someone has made in my life."

Susan's work in marketing communications began in her early twenties after the paper she worked for was sold and the staff was downsized. She was hired by a small public relations firm whose president took her under his wing and gave her extensive training that she equates to receiving an advanced degree. Because she was the only employee, Susan got the opportunity to do a good deal of multitasking, which she describes as very scary but a great learning experience. What she likes most about marketing communications is being able to use her journalistic instincts to develop a strategic plan for a project and then see it all come together.

Susan says that she would not have continued working as a writer if it hadn't been for the encouragement of mentors early in her career. People who were successful in the field told her that she had the talent to become a success herself, and they were honest about how hard she would have to work to make that happen. She says that writing in any form, whether it is novels, Web content, or a newspaper column, is often daunting and solitary, and that feedback is essential.

Susan believes that she wouldn't be as successful as a marketing and communications consultant if she didn't continue to write. She sees the two as interdependent disciplines in her life that nourish one another and provide a positive balance to her work life. She acknowledges, however, that having a dual career is not for everyone. She averages sixty hours a week of billable time but also spends at least another ten hours tending to administrative details such as filing and handling mail, plus another ten or twenty on pro bono projects because she feels that serving as a volunteer adds important balance to her life.

Susan usually begins her day at nine in the morning after a four-mile walk with another writer, with whom she often discusses the day's duties and challenges. They frequently act as each other's editors, which helps greatly because both are sole practitioners. There are also times when Susan works during the night, if she wakes up with an idea or has something she needs to finish.

One of the things Susan most appreciates about working on her own is setting her own schedule, which is determined by what evolves during the day. Despite her best efforts, however, she says that there never seems to be enough time to accomplish everything she wants to do in a given day.

For this reason, Susan has learned to be flexible—if she has a story deadline, she spends the day working on finishing interviews and completing the piece; if she is developing a story, she writes query letters and prepares interview questions. In addition to whatever is on her schedule, she is also working on new ideas for future assignments.

When she is working on a marketing communications project, Susan spends a good deal of time on the phone or doing research. Most of her work is conducted at the computer in her home office. Because she lives in a rural area about an hour from Silicon Valley, Susan tries to maximize her visits to the city by scheduling client meetings, interviews, personal appointments, and errands whenever she visits. She generally spends one day each week out of the office.

Susan offers some advice to others interested in pursuing a dual career such as hers. She says, "I would advise others to seek out internships and really try to get some experience in both these careers before jumping into either one. Education is essential, and so is paying your dues. Marketing communications, even in Silicon Valley, where there are more jobs than people to fill them, is highly competitive. Journalism requires some natural ability going in, as well as a degree."

Kathy Geryk, Newsletter Publisher

Kathy Geryk works out of her home in Connecticut, publishing a monthly newsletter for parents in her community. Although she didn't go to college, Kathy jokes that she has a degree from "The School of Mom."

Kathy began publishing her newsletter, "The Parent Planner" (www.parentplanner.net), because she saw a need for it in her community. Living in a rural area, services are spread out over a large distance, so the newsletter provides a resource for parents and caregivers to find localized information. She didn't have any experience in editing or publishing, but her personal experience as a parent combined with some prior sales experience gave her enough insight into what others raising children need.

Kathy's schedule revolves around her children. After getting them to school in the morning, she works for a few hours either calling clients or going out to meet clients. Once the children are home from school, she stops working except for taking phone calls and then continues to work after the children are in bed, when she edits the paper, contacts clients by e-mail, and writes letters. The schedule works very well for Kathy, allowing her to get her business up and running while still being with her children. She also likes having a tangible sign of her business accomplishments.

Kathy talks honestly about her feelings about working at home. "I really like the fact that each month I have something to call my very own," she says. "Being a parent is difficult in that you don't see your accomplishments on a daily, weekly, or even monthly basis. Everything you do is ruined by the end of the day! You wash the floor and it's dirty again ten minutes later. You do three loads of laundry and three more loads are waiting for you when you are done. Also, when I left my very rewarding career to become a full-time mom, I thought I had lost a lot of myself because I was simply a wife and mother. Although these are titles that I really cherish, I started to wonder where Kathy had gone."

Running the newsletter allows Kathy to have something of her own, and she takes great pride in her work. "The Parent Planner" has even won a national award, which was judged by a panel from the Medill School of Journalism. Kathy competed for the award with hundreds of similar publications from around the country, so her pride is well deserved.

"If I were offering advice to others, I would tell people to never be afraid to try," Kathy says. "You can do anything you want to do and succeed as long as you are willing to put in the time and effort to make it successful."

Creighton D. Barnes, Television Scriptwriter

Creighton Barnes is a television scriptwriter based in Ashland, Oregon. His past work includes projects for Hanna-Barbera, DEC Studios, Marvel Productions, Ruby-Spears Productions, and Mendez-Jenkins Productions in Los Angeles, as well as many studios from Europe, such as European Cinema Productions.

Creighton was interested in writing, so he decided to attend college to prepare for a writing career. Because he was also fascinated by gadgets, he studied engineering. The combination of these two pursuits gave him the technical background to write science fiction. He also loved comics and early cartoons and studied animation production and writing, concentrating on past animators and their scripts. Once he felt ready, he submitted a sample of his writing to a studio head and was hired. He continued writing for the next twenty years.

Creighton credits his newspaper writing and engineering work with giving him the background he uses in his stories. He also feels that his engineering studies helped him to develop the discipline needed to set and achieve goals in his writing.

Today Creighton works from his home. He lives in a secluded mountain area and finds the atmosphere very relaxed (although he does become frustrated when a scene isn't working out as he wants it to). Assignments are posted to an Internet bulletin board that he accesses with a password. When he begins an assignment, Creighton writes a few premises and a one-paragraph synopsis of the story he plans to write. Once the synopsis is accepted, he writes a full outline, which is a scene-by-scene breakdown of the show. Depending on the length of the material, the outline can be from five to twenty pages. After the outline is accepted, he writes the script, which can run from twenty to sixty pages, depending on how much time he has to write it.

Creighton works for five hours in the morning on original material. He takes a break at 1 P.M. and goes to town for lunch and a respite from his office. He returns by 2:30 to work for another four hours, editing and rewriting the previous day's work. Creighton works for about five hours on Saturday, and Sunday is his day off.

Keeping his deadlines in mind, Creighton sets a limit to the number of pages he must write each day to meet the studio's schedule. While this generally works well, his routine can be upset if a story isn't working, and his days might stretch to twelve to fourteen hours until he is back on schedule.

What Creighton enjoys most about his work is the actual writing process and character development, putting his characters into tight spots and watching them find a way out. He says, "It is almost instant gratification seeing your stories come to life weeks (sometimes months) after you have written them. As soon as a script is completed and delivered, you are paid. No waiting."

The downside to Creighton's work is the loneliness, because there is so little contact with others. In addition, he finds that the market is dwindling, although this can be a positive aspect for really talented writers, because only the best will succeed.

Creighton has some specific advice for others considering a screenwriting career. "First, study grammar; know all the parts of speech until you can use them blindfolded and without thinking. Second, read widely; if you are interested in animation, read westerns, science fiction, mainstream novels—everything you can get your hands on. Third, concentrate on the animation industry; learn how things are put together, how cells are made, how many it takes to do a fifteen-minute series (more than seventeen thousand cells), the cost of various activities that go into producing an animation series. Now you are ready to write because you know the high-cost effects, such as showing an opening and closing door, angles that work and those that don't, and so forth.

"Fourth, try to meet people in the industry. Look out for naysayers; they are generally hacks. People close to the industry will know what is coming up and what is hot. This helps when talking one-on-one with a producer who might want to hire you. An animation company will look for these things when you submit your work looking for a job. So will any major studio.

"Finally, keep at it—don't give up. I once kept the head of a major movie studio on the phone for fifteen minutes before he invited me to submit my work to him. I had called from the lobby of the studio, so I took it up to him, we had lunch, and I came away with an assignment. So keep at it. It's difficult to break in, but once you do, everyone will want you."

Blythe Camenson, Freelance Writer, Director of Fiction Writer's Connection

Blythe Camenson received a bachelor of arts degree with a double major in English and psychology from the University of Massachusetts in Boston in 1973 and a master's degree in counseling and education from Northeastern University, Boston, in 1976. Today she is a full-time writer of both nonfiction and fiction, based in Albuquerque, New Mexico. She also serves as director of Fiction Writer's Connection (FWC; www.fictionwriters. com), a membership organization for new and seasoned writers aimed at helping new writers improve their craft and learn the secrets to getting published. Through FWC, she edits a bimonthly newsletter, provides free critiquing to members, and runs a website and a toll-free hotline for member questions. She also organizes and conducts classes and workshops on a variety of topics of interest to writers, including query letter and synopsis writing and approaching editors and agents. To date, she has more than four dozen career books in print, published by McGraw-Hill Trade. Two of her novels have earned movie options, and her articles and photographs have appeared in more than a hundred publications.

"Ever since I read my first Nancy Drew mystery, I knew that I wanted to write," Blythe says, "although it took me a long time before I pursued it professionally. And I always wanted to be my own boss. Writing is the perfect way to do that."

Blythe worked in the Persian Gulf for eight years, teaching English at various universities. She started writing during her last year there, submitting travel articles to local publications and to newspapers and magazines in the United States. In 1990, just before the Gulf War began, she was evacuated out of Baghdad and returned to the United States. Because returning to the Persian Gulf was not an option, she decided to write full-time and began to focus her energy on writing books.

She also started to conduct workshops and arrange writing seminars on a variety of topics featuring guest speakers. While she was overseas, Blythe had to teach herself about writing; she now teaches others through FWC and her website.

Blythe admits that being self-employed might actually be harder than working for someone else. Because she works at home, she tends to work long and odd hours, usually totaling more than forty hours a week. Her schedule is generally to start working early, break for lunch and perhaps a nap, and then return to work in the evening.

While she would like to take weekends off, Blythe finds that there is always something to do, whether it is answering e-mail from new writers, registering new members at FWC, composing newsletters, or attending to website problems.

In addition to the work she does for FWC, Blythe also has deadlines to meet for books she is writing or revising. She prepares for talks she delivers at writers' workshops and conferences and also does editing and critiquing work. Once a given project is complete, there is another one waiting.

Despite the long hours, working on her own in a home office is the biggest perk for Blythe. She appreciates the freedom to organize her own schedule and has to answer only to her editors. She enjoys not having the hassle of a daily commute or dress code to deal with. Blythe also says that while many people find working alone too isolating, she wouldn't be able to write with other people around all the time. So for her, the lack of distractions is a plus.

On the downside, there isn't a regular paycheck, so the monthly income isn't consistent. Like most home-business owners, Blythe pays for her own insurance. Because she is solely responsible for so many projects, there are also very few real vacations.

When asked to offer advice to aspiring writers, Blythe addresses the personal attributes you will need as well as the financial reality of the job. She says, "To have a career as a writer, working for yourself, you have to have a sizable chunk of money to back you up because it takes a long time for those checks to start rolling in. 'Don't quit your day job' is advice often given to new writers. And it's good advice.

"In order to work alone successfully, you need to be very organized and detail oriented, too. You are responsible for everything, from correspondence and filing to making runs to the post office or office supply store. If you tend to procrastinate and object to long hours, you'll find it difficult to work on your own.

"To become successful at writing, you need to learn all the ins and outs of the business. And writing is only half the battle. Marketing your work is the other half."

Joanne Levine, Public Relations Business Owner

Joanne Levine owns Chicago-based Lekas & Levine Public Relations, Inc., which specializes in pursuing media publicity for small and midsize businesses.

Joanne didn't enter the field in the usual way. She majored in English in college, with no ambition to focus on public relations. She joined local community groups while raising her children, and this became a stepping-stone to her future career. While setting up a fund-raiser for one of the organizations, Joanne worked with a public relations professional on the publicity committee.

She learned a lot from the experience and became fascinated by the work.

During this time, Joanne's brother was creating and marketing original adult board games. To test her skills, she wrote and sent out a press release each time he introduced a new game. One game even included Joanne as a character. When the local press picked up the story, she and her brother got both local and national coverage.

"That first project really whetted my appetite," Joanne says. "From there, I began publicizing my husband's retail stores, more civic groups, and the like. One day, I thought about the fact that I was doing a great job and not getting paid for it. I recruited my brother's wife to help me, and we wrote a press release about two sisters-in-law who started a public relations company devoted to small businesses. We got an immediate response from the local chain of newspapers. They wrote a feature article about our company, even though we had no clients. The rest, they say, is history. From that initial article, the phone began to ring, and within a month or two, we had five clients. It's been word of mouth ever since."

In addition to writing copy for brochures and planning special events, Joanne estimates that she spends 80 percent of her time helping clients to appear in newspapers, magazines, and trade publications, as well as on television and radio. Media publicity increases a client's overall visibility and adds credibility to the client's reputation.

Despite the appeal of media publicity to clients, it is not as popular among the public relations professionals who must do the work. As Joanne says, "With an ad, you know what day it will appear, what size it will be, and exactly what it will say. With an article, I hold my breath until the client and I read it in the publication. With a taped interview on radio or television, I wait to see if anything was cut or taken out of context. While my press release and phone conversation with an editor might have been chock-full of the kind of information I hope they will relay to the public, there are no guarantees such as those in advertising. I work with editors and writers who are always on deadline, always overworked, but nevertheless always looking for a good angle. For these reasons, my job can be stressful and sometimes plagued with problems that are completely out of my control."

Despite the pressure, Joanne finds that the positive aspects of her work outweigh the negative. She says, "When all goes well, there's nothing like it. I have seen the positive results of good, steady media campaigns time and time again. And more than once in a while, a really big media appearance can make an overnight difference in someone's business. The client is on cloud nine, his or her phones begin to ring off the hook with new business, and I am showered with praise and gratitude. I often get to know my clients well and enjoy friendly, upbeat working relationships with them. The knowledge that I am helping to make a client's business grow is very rewarding."

Based on her experience, Joanne Levine offers some practical advice for aspiring public relations specialists. "If you want a career in media publicity, I would advise you to read, read, read," she says. "Study the format of newspapers; watch the twelve, five, six, and ten o'clock news. Read every magazine you can get your hands on and note how things are laid out. Reporters have certain 'beats,' and if you can zero in on what they write about, half the battle is won. Familiarizing oneself with the media is a never-ending responsibility. While there are a few good media guides that provide information, this is not a substitute for studying the style of an individual person, section, or publication. Also, as the media faces the same cutbacks and consolidations as any other industry, frequent changes in personnel happen at a rapid pace."

For those seeking a more traditional route, Joanne suggests looking for an internship with a PR company. She has personally used graduate students as freelancers several times.

Joanne stresses that a successful PR person must be original. "Just remember that in order to make it in this field, you need a good imagination and the ability to find an angle," she says. "I can't tell you how many times a client has said, 'I do a better job than anyone else in town and I truly care about my customers.' That's very nice, but it's boring! Find out why the client does a better job. What does he or she do differently? Is the business owner an interesting person? What are his or her hobbies? The list goes on and on. You must be able to pick someone's brain until something newsworthy pops out. Then, you must learn who might be fascinated with your information, so much so that they want to inform their readers about it or share it with their television audience."

Meagan Dawson, Greeting Card Originator and Owner

Meagan Dawson started her own business, Galloping Spirit Greeting Cards, out of her home in Colorado. She earned a bachelor of arts degree in English from the University of Washington and a master's degree in education from Western Washington University.

The company that Meagan worked for previously was bought out, and all employees were laid off. After considering her options, she decided that she wanted to work for herself, creating her own products and running her own business. After months of hard work—designing prototypes, deciding on prices, and building retailer lists—she slowly began to build a profitable business.

Meagan has a lifelong interest in art and poetry. She says, "As an English major, I knew that when you combine the right words in the right order, they can create a masterpiece and literally change people's lives. I want to be a positive influence for my customers, my community, and ultimately the world we live in. Since the inception of my business, I have struggled with designing the perfect pieces of artwork to complement the quotes and poetry. I now feel that the combination of my art and poetry creates a hopeful message to my customers, which is the primary goal of my company."

As a graduate student, Meagan taught English in Spain and Ireland, and this experience helped her to understand the common ideas of beauty shared by different cultures. Her time abroad taught her that we all have dreams, hopes, and expectations, and it is this that she hopes to express through her cards. Meagan also directed a summer writing program for children at the Loveland Museum in Colorado, which reminded her of her love of art and writing and encouraged her to begin planning her business.

Meagan's earlier jobs were at a business seminar company, an aeronautical equipment manufacturer, and an organic foods producer. She acquired her basic business knowledge from all of these jobs, where she learned about marketing, operations, finances, sales, and communications. As a result, she strongly recommends that anyone who plans to start a home-based business takes the time to work full- or part-time for a corporation to gain valuable insight into organization and planning.

Meagan also praises public libraries as "the soul of small businesses." As she says, "Sure, you could buy all your resources at a large bookstore, but libraries save you money and have everything you need to start your small business. I read about ten hours per week, and these books have given me inspiration, advice, and basic knowledge of how the world of business works. Industry knowledge and business sense are required."

Meagan enjoys knowing that, as far as the business is concerned, she is in charge of her fate. If a problem arises, she is responsible for finding the answer. Although it would be nice to pass it along to someone else, she would worry that it wouldn't be handled properly. On some days, it seems that every possible problem occurs, and Meagan must work to solve all of them. On other days, sales are up, production runs smoothly, and she is able to take the next day or two off to spend with her husband. As she says, it's a trade-off that each person needs to consider to decide whether the benefits outweigh the costs.

The best part of running her own business for Meagan is the opportunity to learn and to research. She loves creating a product and seeing the reaction from retailers and their customers. She enjoys knowing that her cards have an impact on people's lives. On the practical side, she likes having the freedom to work when she wants to and to take time off when she needs to. She happily anticipates being a stay-at-home mother when she has children.

For Meagan, the downside of running a home-based business is the financial and emotional risk involved. She can't always project her sales for the next month, and stress at work can take a toll on personal relationships. She also admits that it's hard not to take it personally when people turn away from a product that she designed.

Meagan's advice for others is to research the industry you plan to enter, test your products, and start slowly. "Going to the bank and getting a huge loan does not start a business," she warns. "There are so many aspects that will create a successful project. Time and knowledge are your friends. I would also advise people to choose something that they really love. And I mean really love because you will be eating, sleeping, and living that product for a very long time. Make sure it's something you want to form a deep and meaningful relationship with. All of this takes time—building a business, building your profits, and, ultimately, building a way of life."

Madeline Cohen, Senior Counselor, Public Relations

Madeline Cohen received her associate's degree in applied science from New York City Technical College in 1982, her bachelor of fine arts from New York University of the Arts, and training from the Hilton International Career Development Institute in Montreal in 1983. She is now senior counselor at Patrice Tanaka and Company, a public relations firm in New York City.

After several editorial jobs, Madeline worked as a journalist at a trade publication, where she wrote an article on the Hilton International hotel company. The piece was such a success with Hilton that several months later the public relations director asked to see her about a position in the company's public relations department. She had become so interested in the hotel industry that she even began studying for a degree in hospitality management, so Madeline took the job and stayed with Hilton for ten years while the company underwent several takeovers. Eventually, when she lost her job after the company was sold again, she worked independently in travel public relations.

Madeline decided to work on her own from home and was fortunate to get a lot of business through word-of-mouth advertising. After four years, she was asked to join Patrice Tanaka and Company as a travel industry expert. She commuted for fourteen months and then began to work from home again so she could be with her children. Over time, she has had the opportunity to broaden her expertise into a wide range of consumer products and services with Tanaka.

During the week, Madeline spends seven to nine hours a day working in her home office. Its location at the front of the house helps to ward off any feelings of isolation, because she can watch the world through a large window. Her husband also works from home, so they usually have lunch together. Most of her time is spent at the computer, writing press materials and new business programs and answering e-mail. She also does a good deal of Internet research for current clients and new business proposals.

Madeline describes the pace of her job as very hectic. She generally handles accounts for four clients simultaneously. Accounts involve meetings—often conducted by conference call—with clients, account team, and staff. Research and media contacts are also handled by phone. She says that by the end of a workday, only the "musts" have been taken care of, because there's never enough time to get ahead—as a public relations specialist, she always has a crisis to handle.

Because Madeline is a writer working in public relations, it is the writing and research parts of the job that she likes best. She cares less for the administrative end of the job, such as writing reports and managing deadlines. She feels fortunate to work for an agency that is unique in its willingness to allow her to work on a wide range of projects, doing work that she enjoys. She has a good amount of flexibility, and working at home allows her the freedom to concentrate more on writing and research and less on staff supervision and administration.

Based on her own experience, Madeline offers some thoughtful advice for others considering a telecommuting career. "I would say that once you select your field, work on-site until you develop the expertise needed to become an expert in your field," she says. "Then you can move your work home, either independently or as a staff telecommuter, without ruffling any feathers. If you are doing your work well, people have to accept the fact that you don't need to be on-site to do it. Setting up a home office or business requires organization and dedication to a schedule. It takes about a year to get everything running smoothly. Oh, yes, I'd also recommend that you definitely get a good accountant!"

Carol Page, Freelance Writer

Carol Page is president and owner of Carol Page Communications of Somerville, Massachusetts (www.carolpage.com). She earned a bachelor of arts degree in anthropology from the University of Wisconsin in Madison.

Growing up in a mill town in Wisconsin, Carol dreamed about becoming a writer. All of her writing experience was earned by working. She was determined to be a writer and began to write short articles after college, and she worked as a stringer for the *National Enquirer* for eighteen years.

Although she has published about fifty stories, Carol describes freelance writing as "a very tough profession." She thoroughly enjoys marketing and has a strong entrepreneurial streak but finds it difficult to write material that editors are looking for. So Carol decided to become an editor herself and started "PURRRRR! The Newsletter for Cat Lovers." She wrote some of the material and accepted submissions for the rest. Without an advertising budget, Carol promoted the newsletter herself, appearing on the "Today Show" and NPR's "All Things Considered." She also received positive print coverage in such publications as the *Boston Globe*, *Washington Post*, *Los Angeles Times*, *Chicago Tribune*, *Changing Times*, and *Glamour*.

With this experience, she became a writer and public relations professional and worked in both careers for years. In recent years, she has focused exclusively on public relations, which is much more lucrative. She started Carol Page Communications in 1998.

Carol's work experience gave her a good deal of insight into her new career. She says, "Having been a journalist for so long, I knew that the media relations part of public relations was really just reverse journalism. I'd had hundreds of press kits pass over my desk that had been pitched by many public relations professionals. I knew what the press needed because I was one of them. Now, when a potential client asks me to tell me about myself, I begin with, 'I am a recovering journalist.'"

Carol enjoys working in public relations. When a project is going well, she finds great pleasure in strategizing with clients to help them promote their product or service. She loves the fact that as she helps a client's business grow, her own business grows as well. She's fascinated by the public relations business, which has its own brand of creativity.

On a typical day, Carol spends most of her time on the telephone and sending e-mail. She describes her job as talking people into doing things, whether it is to use a client's product or to hire her to promote their own business. Based on her experience, Carol believes that public relations work requires a good deal of skill and maturity. She feels that she would not have been as successful in the field when she was younger, because she lacked the sophistication and experience to fully appreciate a client's needs.

Some days are slower than others; some days are extremely busy. What Carol appreciates most about working in a home office is that she can generally set the pace herself. She can monitor calls if she needs to concentrate on a project. If she really needs a break, she might go to a movie. But she never really takes a day off, working between sixty and seventy hours a week. Although she may not work all the time, Carol finds that when she is home, she is usually doing something work-related. As she says, "I tried to take a vacation at home once and found myself organizing new rolodexes and file systems. The only way to take time off is literally to go away. I'm very interested in what I do, so I think about it a lot, even when picking out soy sauce in the supermarket."

As much as Carol loves her work, she admits that dealing with clients is not always easy. Sometimes a client doesn't appreciate the job that's been done for them, which Carol attributes to their not understanding the significance of the work. Many potential clients are really unaware of what public relations is and don't fully understand what Carol can do for them, and working with them can be difficult.

Carol has some brief but sound advice for aspiring home-business owners. "My advice for others considering starting their own home-based businesses: Don't get too comfortable. Keep looking for new business all the time, even if you have all you can handle. Clients come and go in a flash."

Wade Hyde, Publicist and Professional Writer

Wade Hyde earned his bachelor of science degree in radio, television, and film from the University of Texas at Austin in 1985. He received the Outstanding Student Award from the College of

Communication's Department of Radio-Television-Film. He is now a partner in Wade Hyde Corporation (www.wadehyde.com) in Dallas, Texas.

Wade's background spans more than a decade of diversified corporate communications, public relations, and investor relations experience, including working with several nationally recognized companies and organizations, such as Blockbuster Video; FoxMeyer Corporation (now McKesson), a $5.5 billion pharmaceutical distribution company; Anthem Health (now Ameri-Health), a Blue Cross/Blue Shield–affiliated organization; and television stations CBS-affiliate KDFW-TV and independent KXTX-TV. Most recently Hyde served as vice president of marketing and public relations for a publicly traded real estate investment company.

Wade sees marketing and public relations as primarily about communication, the way people relate to each other. However, good communication skills are best when coupled with another strong ability. Encouraged by his father, an executive recruiter, to minor in a subject that had professional marketability, Wade chose computer science. He believes that this is one of the best decisions he has ever made, because most of his early employment opportunities were based on his computer skills. Today, the combination of his work experience and technical and communication skills allow him to succeed beyond others without such a strong background.

Wade spends much of his time corresponding by e-mail and telephone. He describes the computer, telephone, and fax machines as the lifelines of his business. He says, "Since I'm a publicist and a professional writer, I write and talk and talk about my writing." Wade describes himself as a telecommuting subcontractor and is glad to be free of the hour commute he used to have between home and office. He usually works from 8:30 A.M. to 5:30 P.M., with an hour break for lunch. He does set his own schedule, though, and sometimes will work late or start later in the morning. On occasion he might mow the lawn in the afternoon or do his grocery shopping.

Wade finds telecommuting to be ideal for personal and professional flexibility and feels that he works more efficiently now than before, yet has more personal freedom and less pressure. It is the flexibility that he likes most about his job. Wade doesn't find any significant downside to his situation. While he acknowledges that he could probably earn more money working as a corporate vice president in an office setting, he would rather have the personal and professional freedom that he enjoys working from home.

Wade offers some succinct advice to other home-based workers. He says, "Regardless of your career choice, be technically astute, especially if you'll be telecommuting or working on your own. Otherwise, you can't compete against the larger office-based companies."

Lisa Achilles, Senior Account Executive in Public Relations

Lisa Achilles received a bachelor of arts degree in communications from Auburn University in Alabama in 1989. Today she works from her home in Gainesville, Georgia, as a senior account executive for Katcher Vaughn & Bailey (www.kvbpr.com), based in Nashville, Tennessee.

Lisa has always enjoyed writing and knew that she wanted a career that would allow her to use her writing skills. She began working as a reporter with a small newspaper in Callahan, Florida. She was recommended for the job by the editor of her hometown newspaper in Georgia. After working as a reporter for a few years, she and her husband relocated and she decided to try a new career. She took a position at a public relations agency and loved the work.

Her introduction to public relations came in college, where Lisa served as a hostess for the athletic department. She assisted in football recruiting, escorting high school players who were invited to visit the college. Her responsibilities included giving tours of the athletic facilities, spending time with recruits and their families, and generally promoting the school. In retrospect, Lisa equates trying to persuade the recruits to accept football scholarships to public relations professionals trying to persuade the media to cover their clients.

In her current job, Lisa writes press releases, advertising copy, brochures, and newsletters. She also talks to the media about news from her clients and encourages the media to run stories about them. She finds that her reporting experience is an asset in pitching stories to the media, because it gives her a better understanding of which stories might be picked up and which are unlikely to get attention.

Lisa enjoys the excitement of working for a public relations agency, where no two days are ever the same. When a client has a crisis, she must stop everything else to handle it. Despite the occasional craziness, Lisa likes being faced with the unexpected as opposed to working within a fixed schedule.

Her present situation is less stressful, however, because she works part-time, putting in about twenty hours a week. Lisa finds that she is more relaxed and therefore more productive. She works in an upstairs office with a computer, printer, fax machine, and telephone. There are no distractions, which helps her concentration and productivity.

Lisa particularly enjoys working with start-up companies, those with small budgets and little money for advertising. Public relations is crucial to such companies, which need publicity to become known in their industry. Lisa finds it rewarding to see a start-up client grow into a successful business and to know that her work has contributed to that success.

The only downside that Lisa finds in her work is occasional uncertainty. For example, she and her colleagues might work on a story for months only to learn that it has been bumped at the last minute due to a breaking news story. Although this is frustrating, it can't get in the way of producing the best promotion for the client.

Lisa's advice to others is simple. She says, "To be successful doing this kind of work, I would say you have to be very organized, a good writer, a fast thinker, and able to work under deadlines. You also have to be able to handle rejection and criticism."

The Communications Path

Our able communicators—Karen L. Sullivan, Susan Ditz, Kathy Geryk, Creighton D. Barnes, Blythe Camenson, Joanne Levine, Meagan Dawson, Madeline Cohen, Carol Page, Wade Hyde, and Lisa Achilles—show us a wide range of backgrounds and experiences. Though their circumstances were, in many cases, quite different, they all found success as home-based communicators—many specializing in public relations. Their experiences demonstrate that no matter what your personal circumstances are, no matter what area of the country you live in, and no matter what your education or training might be, you have the potential to become a successful home-based careerist.

eBay for Homebodies

Business is not financial science, it's about trading . . . buying and selling. It's about creating a product or service so good that people will pay for it.
—Anita Roddick

When you think of starting a home-based business, it's quite likely that eBay will come to mind as a possibility for your venture. You've heard the many success stories of people making good money selling items on the auction site—perhaps this is an option for your new business.

Getting Started

One of the attractions of starting a business on eBay is that you really don't need much business experience. The site is very well organized, and if you spend enough time browsing, you'll become familiar with the ins and outs. There is even eBay University, which offers sessions nationwide thirty weekends a year; each session accommodates up to seven hundred attendees. Two courses are offered: a day-long session that teaches the basics of selling and an advanced class that teaches tips to help experienced sellers increase their sales.

The site also offers an online community where sellers can join chat groups and exchange ideas and advice, as well as a mentoring program that pairs established sellers with small groups of new sellers. Other groups allow sellers to meet in person. There's even an online group that includes women who sell on eBay as full-time jobs.

Because you can sell nearly anything on eBay, take some time to think about the items you'd like to offer. It's easy to get carried away by the success of others, so be sure to give this as much thought for your eBay business as you would for any other kind of business. It's wise to choose an area you're familiar with—perhaps you worked for years in the music industry or as a teacher—and sell items that relate to that profession. Most people initially get some practice by selling unwanted household items or gifts they can't use. This will help you to get a feel for the process and learn what works and what doesn't. It's also a way to earn some money that can go toward your purchase of the items you intend to sell in your business.

Tips for Success

The following pointers, adapted from an article in *Entrepreneur* *.com*, are intended to help you organize your eBay business in the most profitable way.[1]

- **Select a user ID.** Your user ID will represent your business to buyers. Some become quite well known, so choose yours carefully.
- **Take the "How to Sell" tour.** Take advantage of the site's learning tools. Watch the selling demonstration video, and visit the eBay learning center.

[1] "19 eBay Success Secrets," *Entrepreneur.com*, September 7, 2005, www.entrepreneur.com/article/0,4621,323280,00.html.

- **Use the "ID Verify" option.** You can use this either instead of or in addition to giving credit card information when you set up your seller's account. Using the ID Verify option will give you an eBay icon, which many buyers look for when selecting items to purchase.
- **Use accounting software.** A good accounting software program will let you keep track of how the business is doing financially. It can also help you keep track of customers and vendors and can be a great help when preparing your tax returns.
- **Back up your hard drive.** Make it a habit to save all of your business information on disks or CDs. This goes for documents and your accounting records. Label everything carefully and store the CDs in a safe place.
- **Choose your selling category.** Click the "Buy" button on the eBay home page to browse selling categories. Find what works best for the items you plan to sell. You might consider choosing two categories in order to reach more buyers.
- **Don't forget the fees.** eBay charges small fees for listing and selling your items, which you should consider when setting a price for your items.
- **Highlight your listings.** For a fee, you can attract buyers by adding a color highlight or border to your listing or by adding a subtitle that includes additional information about the item.
- **Use "My eBay."** The "My eBay" feature lets you monitor your listings and activity. The "My Messages" option helps you keep track of any eBay correspondence.
- **Hire an assistant.** Once your eBay business is up and running, you might consider hiring a trading assistant to help manage your listings—this will let you focus on other

aspects of the business and keep from becoming swamped by handling trades. For information about finding a trading assistant, click "Sell" on the eBay home page, then go to "Find a local trading assistant."

- **Keep a to-do list.** It helps to keep a daily list of activities and responsibilities that require your attention. It's a good idea to leave some time each day to handle any unscheduled tasks that come up.

- **Make room for inventory and materials.** You'll need to find a safe, dry place to store your inventory items and shipping materials. You can obtain free eBay-USPS cobranded Priority Mail shipping boxes from the U.S. Postal Service. Order them at http://ebaysupplies.usps.com.

- **Ask the pros for advice.** eBay consultants are available to answer your questions and offer free advice on how to make your business profitable. The "Seller OnRamp" will link you with consultants who can help you.

- **Subscribe to the "Chatter."** This monthly spot offers articles, tips, links, and member interviews.

- **Sign up for the "PowerUp Newsletter."** You'll receive advance notice by e-mail of upcoming events and promotions, including discounts, seller sweepstakes, free listing days, and more.

- **Market your store.** Business cards, fliers, letterhead, and newsletters can all help to reinforce your brand and make it noticeable to more buyers. Visit the "Promote your store" page for details. You can also create and mail promotional materials through the U.S. Postal Service's NetPost Business Connect site.

- **Watch for unusual buyer requests.** Be alert to unusual requests, such as buyers who ask to send partial payments.

- **Attend industry trade shows.** Trade shows give you a preview of coming trends and let you interact with manufacturers to discuss selling possibilities. Go to the trade shows prepared to market your store—bring business cards and other promotional materials and your confidence as a successful seller.
- **Donate to a nonprofit organization.** You can donate some or all of an item's final sale price to nonprofit organizations. Your charity listings will be highlighted with a blue and yellow ribbon icon, letting buyers know that you support the community.

With these tips in mind, you have the foundation to get your eBay business off to a running start. But be sure to treat this as you would any other business—although initially it might seem more like fun than work, it's still a real business. You'll need to apply for any licenses or permits that your state imposes on other home-based ventures. Stress can still be a factor, especially if you're working alone—you'll be responsible for finding and marketing items, handling trades, shipping items, and keeping track of it all. Taking care of yourself is a good way to take care of business.

Resources for More Information

The following associations, agencies, and websites are good sources of additional information about starting a home-based business. The Internet has become a remarkable resource for learning about virtually any field of endeavor, and most organizations and large businesses provide detailed information on their websites.

Associations and Agencies

American Entrepreneurs for Economic Growth (AEEG)
1655 North Fort Myer Drive, Suite 850
Arlington, VA 22209
www.aeeg.org

American Home Business Association
1981 East Murray-Holladay Road, Suite 225
Salt Lake City, UT 84117
www.homebusiness.com

American Institute of Small Business
426 Second Street
Excelsior, MN 55331
www.101bizclasses.com

American Telecommuting Association
1220 L Street NW, Suite 100
Washington, DC 20005
www.knowledgetree.com

Canadian Association of Women Executives and
   Entrepreneurs
PO Box 620
Station P
Toronto, ON M5S 2Y4
Canada
www.cawee.net

Canadian Chamber of Commerce
Delta Office Tower
350 Sparks Street, Suite 501
Ottawa, ON K1R 7S8
Canada
www.chamber.ca

Canada Small Business Financing Program
Industry Canada
C.D. Howe Building
235 Queen Street, Eighth Floor East
Ottawa, ON K1A 0H5
Canada
http://strategis.ic.gc.ca/epic/internet/
   incsbfp-pfpec.nsf/en/Home

Canadian Telework Association
5749 Doyle Road
Ottawa, ON K4M 1B4
Canada
www.ivc.ca

Canadian Youth Business Foundation
100 Adelaide Street West, Suite 1410
Toronto, ON M5H 1S3
www.cybf.ca

Edward Lowe Foundation
58220 Decatur Road
PO Box 8
Cassopolis, MI 49031
http://edwardlowe.org

Home-Based Working Moms
PO Box 500164
Austin, TX 78750
www.hbwm.com

Home Office Association of America
909 Third Avenue, Suite 990
New York, NY 10022
www.hoaa.com

Industry Canada
Minister of Industry
Fifth Floor, West Tower
C.D. Howe Building
235 Queen Street
Ottawa, ON K1A 0H5
Canada
www.ic.gc.ca

International Franchise Association
1501 K Street NW, Suite 530
Washington, DC 20005
www.franchise.org

Minority Business Development Agency (MBDA)
U.S. Department of Commerce
1401 Constitution Avenue NW
Washington, DC 20230
www.mbda.gov

Mother's Home Business Network
PO Box 423
East Meadow, NY 11554
www.homeworkingmom.com

My Own Business
13181 Crossroads Parkway North, Suite 190
City of Industry, CA 91746
www.myownbusiness.org

National Association of Women Business Owners
8405 Greensboro Drive, Suite 800
McLean, VA 22101
www.nawbo.org

National Association for the Self-Employed (NASE)
PO Box 612067
DFW Airport
Dallas, TX 75261
www.nase.org

National Business Association (NBA)
5151 Beltline Road, Suite 1150
Dallas, TX 75370
www.nationalbusiness.org

National Federation of Independent Businesses (NFIB)
53 Century Boulevard, Suite 205
Nashville, TN 37214
www.nfibonline.com

National Small Business Association
1156 Fifteenth Street NW, Suite 1100
Washington, DC 20005
www.nsba.biz

Office of Advocacy
U.S. Small Business Administration
409 Third Street, Seventh Floor
Washington, DC 20416
www.sba.gov/advo

Office of Women Business Ownership
U.S. Small Business Administration
409 Third Street SW
Washington, DC 20416
www.sba.gov/women

Patent and Trademark Office
U.S. Department of Commerce
1401 Constitution Avenue NW
Washington, DC 20230
www.uspto.gov

Service Corps of Retired Executives (SCORE)
409 Third Street SW, Sixth Floor
Washington, DC 20024
www.score.org

Small Business Advancement National Center
University of Central Arkansas
College of Business Administration
UCA Box 5018
201 Donaghey Avenue
Conway, AR 72035
www.sbaer.uca.edu

U.S. Association of Small Business and Entrepreneurship
DeSantis Center, Suite 207
Florida Atlantic University
College of Business
777 Colades Road, Building 87, Room 207F
Boca Raton, FL 33431
www.usasbe.org

U.S. Chamber of Commerce
1615 H Street NW
Washington, DC 20062
www.uschamber.com

U.S. Copyright Office
101 Independence Avenue SE
Washington, DC 20559
www.copyright.gov

U.S. Department of Commerce (DOC)
1401 Constitution Avenue NW
Washington, DC 20230
www.commerce.gov

U.S. Small Business Administration (SBA)
409 Third Street SW
Washington, DC 20416
www.sba.gov

Websites

BPlans.com
www.bplans.com
> *A collection of information and sample business plans for small to midsize businesses*

Canada One
www.canadaone.com
> *Resource site for small-business owners and entrepreneurs*

Entrepreneur.com
www.entrepreneur.com
> *Information about all aspects of entrepreneurship*

Franchise.com
www.franchise.com
> *Information on selecting, purchasing, and running a franchise*

Home-Based Business Suite
www.smallbusinessadvocate.com
> *Articles on all aspects of home-based business*

MoreBusiness.com
www.morebusiness.com
Entrepreneurs share information and resources

National Association of Home-Based Businesses (NAHBB)
www.usahomebusiness.com
Information on business opportunities, marketing, and other aspects of business

Online Women's Business Center
www.onlinewbc.gov
Information for women business owners

PureBusiness.com
www.purebusiness.com
Information about incorporation, domain registration, and financial issues

Small Business Advancement National Center
www.sbaer.uca.edu
Resources for small-business owners and entrepreneurs

Small Business and Self-Employed One-Stop Resource
www.irs.gov/businesses/small
IRS information for the self-employed and small-business owners

Small Business Computing
www.smallbusinesscomputing.com
Technology-based information for the small-business owner

Small, Minority, and Women-Owned Business Resources
www.proposalwriter.com/small.html
Information on government funding, business plans, and general resources

SOHO America (Small Office Home Office)
www.soho.org
Resources for marketing, financial and legal issues, and technology

Working Solo, Inc.
www.workingsolo.com
Information regarding business, mentors, and general resources

Suggested Reading

There are many publications available that offer information and guidance on all aspects of running a home-based business. The following books and magazines are just a sampling of what is available.

Books

Bond, Robert E. *Bond's Top 100 Franchises: An In-Depth Analysis of Today's Top Franchise Opportunities*, 2nd ed. Oakland, CA: Source Book Publications, 2005.

Chaston, Ian. *Small Business e-Commerce Management*. New York: Palgrave Macmillan, 2004.

Daily, Frederick W., and Bethany K. Laurence. *Tax Savvy for Small Business: Year-Round Tax Strategies to Save You Money*, 9th ed. Berkeley, CA: NOLO, 2005.

Davis, Martin E. *Managing a Small Business Made Easy*. New York: Entrepreneur Press, 2005.

Dodd, Pamela, and Doug Sundheim. *The 25 Best Time Management Tools & Techniques: How to Get More Done Without Driving Yourself Crazy*. Peak Performance Press, 2005.

Eker, T. Harv. *Secrets of the Millionaire Mind: Mastering the Inner Game of Wealth*. New York: HarperCollins, 2005.

Farrell, Larry C. *Getting Entrepreneurial!: Creating and Growing Your Own Business in the 21st Century—Lessons from the World's Greatest Entrepreneurs*. New York: John Wiley & Sons, 2003.

Feig, Barry. *Streetwise Low-Cost Web Site Promotion: Every Possible Way to Make Your Web Site a Success, Without Spending Lots of Money.* Avon, MA: Adams Media Corp., 2001.

Fishman, Stephen. *Working for Yourself: Law & Taxes for Independent Contractors, Freelancers & Consultants,* 6th ed. Berkeley, CA: NOLO, 2006.

Florzak, Douglas. *The Free Agent Marketing Guide: 100+ Marketing Tips for Free Agents, Independent Consultants, and Freelancers.* Westmont, IL: Logical Directions, 2004.

Gilbert, Jill. *The Entrepreneur's Guide to Patents, Copyrights, Trademarks, Trade Secrets & Licensing.* New York: Berkley Trade, 2004.

Ginsberg, Adam. *How to Buy, Sell, and Profit on eBay: Kick-Start Your Home-Based Business in Just Thirty Days.* New York: HarperCollins, 2005.

Harvard Business School Press. *Time Management: Increase Your Personal Productivity and Effectiveness.* Cambridge, MA: Harvard Business School Press, 2005.

Hisrich, Robert D. *Small Business Solutions: How to Fix and Prevent the 13 Biggest Problems That Derail Business.* New York: McGraw-Hill, 2004.

Goliszek, Andrew. *60 Second Stress Management: The Quickest Way to Relax and Ease Anxiety.* Far Hills, NJ: New Horizon Press, 2004.

Huff, Priscilla. *101 Best Home-Based Businesses for Women: Everything You Need to Know About Getting Started on the Road to Success,* 3rd ed. New York: Three Rivers Press, 2002.

Hupalo, Peter I. *Getting Rich in Your Underwear: How to Start and Run a Profitable Home-Based Business.* West St. Paul, MN: HCM Publishing, 2005.

Kanarek, Lisa. *Home Office Solutions: Creating a Space That Works for You.* Bloomington, IN: Quarry Books, 2004.

Keup, Erwin J. *Franchise Bible.* New York: Entrepreneur Press, 2004.

Koenig, Steve, and Hal Root. *The Small Business Start-Up Guide*. Naperville, IL: Sourcebooks, Inc., 2005.

Leland, Karen, and Keith Bailey. *Customer Service for Dummies*, 3rd ed. New York: Wiley Publishing, Inc., 2006.

Levonsky, Rieva. *Start Your Own Business*, 3rd ed. New York: Entrepreneur Press, 2004.

Malta, Chris, and Lisa Suttora. *What to Sell on eBay and Where to Get It*. New York: McGraw-Hill, 2006.

McGarvey, Robert, and Melissa Campanelli. *Start Your Own e-Business*. New York: Entrepreneur Press, 2005.

McQuown, Judith H. *Inc. Yourself: How to Profit by Setting Up Your Own Corporation*, 10th ed. Franklin Lakes, NJ: Career Press, 2004.

Meaney, James A. *How to Buy a Franchise*, 2nd ed. Naperville, IL: Sphinx Publishing, 2004.

Miller, Michael. *Absolute Beginner's Guide to Launching an eBay Business*. Indianapolis: Que, 2003.

Patsula, Peter J. *Successful Business Planning in 30 Days: A Step-By-Step Guide for Writing a Business Plan and Starting Your Own Business*, 3rd ed. Mansfield, OH: Patsula Media, 2004.

Pinson, Linda. *Anatomy of a Business Plan: A Step-by-Step Guide to Building a Business and Securing Your Company's Future*, 6th ed. New York: Kaplan Business, 2004.

Pinson, Linda. *Keeping the Books: Basic Record Keeping and Accounting for the Successful Small Business*, 6th ed. New York: Kaplan Business, 2004.

Reese, Harvey. *How to License Your Million Dollar Idea: Everything You Need to Know to Turn a Simple Idea into a Million Dollar Payday*, 2nd ed. New York: Wiley Publishing, Inc., 2002.

Reynolds, Janice. *The Complete E-Commerce Book: Design, Build, and Maintain a Successful Web-Based Business*. Gilroy, CA: CMP Books, 2004.

Schenck, Barbara F. *Small Business Marketing for Dummies*, 2nd ed. New York: Wiley Publishing, Inc., 2005.

Schepp, Debra, and Brad Schepp. *eBay Powerseller Secrets: Insider Tips from eBay's Most Successful Sellers.* Emeryville, CA: McGraw-Hill/Osborne, 2004.

Sinclair, Joseph T. *eBay Business the Smart Way: Maximize Your Profits on the Web's #1 Auction Site,* 2nd ed. New York: AMACOM, 2004.

Stephenson, James. *Ultimate Small Business Marketing Guide.* New York: Entrepreneur Press, 2003.

Strauss, Steven B. *The Small Business Bible: Everything You Need to Know to Succeed in Your Small Business.* New York: John Wiley & Sons, 2004.

Sweeney, Susan. *101 Internet Businesses You Can Start from Home.* Gulf Breeze, FL: Maximum Press, 2001.

Timm, Paul R. *50 Powerful Ideas You Can Use to Keep Your Customers,* 3rd ed. Franklin Lakes, NJ: Career Press, 2002.

Tyson, Eric, and Jim Schell. *Small Business for Dummies,* 2nd ed. New York: Wiley Publishing, Inc., 2003.

Williams, Robin, and John Tollett. *The Non-Designer's Web Book,* 3rd ed. Berkeley, CA: Peachpit Press, 2005.

Winner, Jay, and Susan Myers. *Stress Management Made Simple: Effective Ways to Beat Stress for Better Health.* Santa Barbara, CA: Blue Fountain Press, 2003.

Zetlin, Minda. *Telecommuting for Dummies.* New York: Hungry Minds, 2001.

Zobel, Jan. *Minding Her Own Business: The Self-Employed Woman's Essential Guide to Taxes and Financial Records,* 4th ed. Naperville, IL: Sphinx Publishing, 2005.

Zoglio, Suzanne W. *Recharge in Minutes: The Quick-Lift Way to Less Stress, More Success, and Renewed Energy.* Doylestown, PA: Tower Hill Press, 2003.

Magazines (Print and Online)

Enterprise Magazine (Canada)
www.enterprisemag.com

Fortune Small Business
http://money.cnn.com/magazines/fsb

Home Business Magazine
www.homebusinessmag.com

Home Office
http://entrepreneur.com/homebasedbiz

Inc.com
www.inc.com

My Business
www.mybusinessmag.com

PC Magazine Small Business Supersite
www.pcmag.com/category2/0,4148,13806,00.asp

Small Business Opportunities
www.sbomag.com

Small Business Technology
www.sbtechnologymagazine.org

Telecommuting Review
www.gilgordon.com/review/index.htm

WAHM.com
www.wahm.com
   Magazine for work-at-home mothers

About the Author

Jan Goldberg's love for the printed page began well before her second birthday. Regular visits to the bookbindery where her grandfather worked produced a magic combination of sights and smells that she carries with her to this day.

Childhood was filled with composing poems and stories, reading books, and playing library. Elementary and high school included an assortment of contributions to school newspapers. While a full-time college student, Goldberg wrote extensively as part of her job responsibilities in the College of Business Administration at Roosevelt University in Chicago. After receiving a degree in elementary education, she was able to extend her love of reading and writing to her students.

Goldberg has written extensively in the occupations area for *Weekly Reader* magazine for middle school and high school students, as well as for the many career publications produced by Cass Communications. She has also contributed to a number of projects for educational publishers, including Free Spirit Publishing, Capstone Publishing, Publications International, Scott Foresman, Addison-Wesley, and Camp Fire Boys and Girls. She recently coauthored the revised and updated edition of *Perfectionism: What's Bad About Being Too Good?*, which was named to the New York Library's list of the best "Books for the Teen Age" for the year 2000.

As a feature writer, Goldberg's work has appeared in *Parenting Magazine, Today's Chicago Woman, Opportunity Magazine, Chicago Parent, Correspondent, Successful Student, Complete Woman, North Shore Magazine,* and the Pioneer Press newspapers.

In all, she has published more than four hundred pieces as a full-time freelance writer.

In addition to *Careers for Homebodies and Other Independent Souls*, she is the author of nineteen other career books published by McGraw-Hill.

Goldberg also frequently serves as a writing teacher and workshop leader.